THE CIVIL RIGHTS
ACT OF 1964

AN END TO RACIAL SEGREGATION

MILESTONES
IN
AMERICAN HISTORY

MILESTONES
IN
AMERICAN HISTORY

THE CIVIL RIGHTS ACT OF 1964

AN END TO RACIAL SEGREGATION

JUDY L. HASDAY

CHELSEA HOUSE
PUBLISHERS

An imprint of Infobase Publishing

Cover: Martin Luther King Jr. (lower left-hand corner) walks with supporters during the March on Washington on August 28, 1963. Shortly after this photo was taken, King delivered his "I Have a Dream" speech, which laid the groundwork for the Civil Rights Act of 1964.

The Civil Rights Act of 1964: An End to Racial Segregation

Copyright © 2007 by Infobase Publishing

Chelsea House
An imprint of Infobase Publishing
132 West 31st Street
New York NY 10001

ISBN-10: 0-7910-9355-7
ISBN-13: 978-0-7910-9355-9

Library of Congress Cataloging-in-Publication Data
Hasday, Judy L., 1957-
  The Civil Rights Act of 1964 : an end to racial segregation / Judy L. Hasday.
      p. cm. — (Milestones in American History)
  Includes bibliographical references and index.
  ISBN 0-7910-9355-7 (hardcover)
  1. Civil rights—United States—History—20th century. 2. United States. Civil Rights Act of 1964. 3. African Americans—Civil rights—History—20th century. 4. Segregation—Law and legislation—United States—History—20th century. I. Title.
  KF4749.H36 2007
  342.7308'509046—dc22   2006038702

Chelsea House books are available at special discounts when purchased in bulk quantities for businesses, associations, institutions, or sales promotions. Please call our Special Sales Department in New York at (212) 967-8800 or (800) 322-8755.

You can find Chelsea House on the World Wide Web at http://www.chelseahouse.com

Series design by Erik Lindstrom
Cover design by Ben Peterson

Printed in the United States of America

Bang NMSG 10 9 8 7 6 5 4 3 2 1

This book is printed on acid-free paper.

All links and Web addresses were checked and verified to be correct at the time of publication. Because of the dynamic nature of the Web, some addresses and links may have changed since publication and may no longer be valid.

CONTENTS

"We the People . . ."

The founding of the United States is one that was based upon the premise of creating a society where all men would live free of persecution and oppression, and where the government would protect the principles of justice and equality for every citizen. And though the first Europeans to arrive on America's shores were primarily explorers and, later, conquerors, by the seventeenth century, Europeans began heading to the New World with the hope of establishing a new home and a new life. It was in America where they hoped to escape political oppression, were free to practice their religion, and make a better life for themselves and their families—all of which was denied them in their homeland.

These same people, who looked to a world where they could be free of the very oppressions they left behind, began to do the same to the peoples already in America—the Native

Americans who lived throughout the sprawling woods, countrysides, and plains of the pristine, undeveloped continent. As more and more immigrants arrived in America, more and more land was "settled," occupied, developed, and exploited for the food and resources necessary to make a living and flourish in the new homeland. As the settlers expanded their territory, they took away the lands upon which the Native Americans had so freely lived. Aggression led to violence, and the Native Americans, ultimately no match for their enemy, were either killed or rounded up and confined to small areas of land known as reservations. The Europeans, once the oppressed, had become the oppressors.

SLAVERY'S BEGINNINGS

Slavery is defined as "the condition in which one person, known as a slave, is under the control of another. Slavery almost always occurs for the purpose of securing the *labour* of the slave. A specific form, known as *chattel slavery*, is defined by the absolute *legal ownership* of a person or persons, including the legal right to buy and sell them just as one would a lamp or an article of clothing."[1] Slavery is as old as civilization itself. More powerful and dominent groups or cultures have enslaved their captured enemies, usually peoples of different races, ethnicities, religions, and often poorer and less able to defend themselves.

The history of African slavery and the development of America are inexorably linked and can be traced to the exploration of the New World by the Spanish in the 1500s. By the 1600s, the African slavery trade was a profitable venture for European ship merchants sailing to Africa and the New World. At drop-off ports in Africa, native peoples were enslaved and brought to Santa Domingo, today the capital city of the Dominican Republic, a nation in the Caribbean Sea. Unlike former slaves in history who served such diverse purposes as warriors, servants, and ritual sacrifice offerings to gods, slaves in the New World were primarily used as a means of forced labor.

By the 1660s, demand for plantation labor in the southern colonies was growing rapidly. To meet this demand, Africans were forcibly brought to America in shackles and made to endure a lifetime of servitude.

The first black Africans were brought to Virginia in 1619, just 12 years after the founding of the Jamestown settlement. At first, many were regarded as indentured servants who could earn their freedom. By the 1660s, however, as the demand for plantation labor in the southern colonies grew, the institution of slavery began to harden around them. Before long, Africans were being brought to America in shackles for a lifetime of involuntary servitude. Slavery had become prominent in the colonies by the time of the beginning of the American Revolution. In declaring their independence, the colonists proclaimed within the lines of the Declaration of Independence that

> When, in the Course of human Events, it becomes necessary for one People to dissolve the Political Bonds which have connected them with another, and to assume, among the Powers of the Earth, the separate and equal Station to which the Laws of Nature and of Nature's God entitle them, a decent Respect to the Opinions of Mankind requires that they should declare the Causes which impel them to the Separation.[2]

For African Americans, choosing sides—independence from Great Britain or remaining under colonial rule of the British Crown—did not matter. What mattered was which group, the Patriots or the Loyalists, would promise them their freedom. The British did actively recruit slaves belonging to Patriot slave masters, with the promise of freedom at war's end. As a result, more blacks fought for the Crown than for American independence. Whichever side they chose, by the end of the war, about 100,000 African Americans had escaped, died, or had been killed. In November 1782, Great Britain and the Patriots—now known as Americans—signed the first draft of a treaty granting the former colonists their independence. As part of the Treaty of Paris, the British were required to return all American property. That included all runaway slaves.

ESPOUSING LIBERTY, PRACTICING BONDAGE

Despite the colonists winning independence, a new and free country meant little to African Americans, for as soon as the war was over they were rounded up and reenslaved. Even more ironic was what the author of the Declaration of Independence, Thomas Jefferson (a slave owner himself), wrote in the introduction to the declaration:

> We hold these truths to be self-evident, that all men are created equal, that they are endowed by their Creator with certain unalienable Rights, that among these are Life, Liberty and the pursuit of Happiness.[3]

These words, part of what has become the cornerstone of American law, did not apply to the slaves living in the United States. In fact, despite an antislavery movement that was gaining some support in the North after the American Revolution, slave owners in the South (where the majority of slaves lived) reasserted their rights to own slaves. They included many compromises in addressing the slavery issue during the revision of the Articles of Confederation at the Constitutional Convention in 1787. Delegates from Georgia and South Carolina even insisted on having a portion of their slave population included when determining representation in Congress. Delegates from the South also won a guarantee that the slave trade—a deplorable process in the eyes of many—would continue unabated for another 20 years.

The word slavery does not appear anywhere in the Constitution, but four key provisions dealt with the issue. The most glaring, Article IV, Section 2 (which was later superseded by the Thirteenth Amendment), states:

> No person held to service or labor in one State, under the laws thereof, escaping into another, shall, in consequence of

any law or regulation therein, be discharged from such service or labor, but shall be delivered up on claim of the party to whom such service or labor may be due.[4]

African Americans were still viewed and treated as property. "Inalienable rights . . ." "Life, liberty, and the pursuit of happiness . . ." "We hold these truths to be self-evident . . ."—these words did not apply to the more than 500,000 slaves living in the United States.

There were problems with the way Article IV, Section 2 was written, as discussed in the PBS program *Africans in America*:

> Although Article IV, Section 2 of the United States Constitution guaranteed the right to repossess any "person held to service or labor" [a euphemism for slaves], it did not set up a mechanism for executing the law. On February 12, 1793, the Second Congress passed "An act respecting fugitives from justice, and persons escaping from the service of their masters," that authorized the arrest or seizure of fugitives and empowered "any magistrate of a county, city or town" to rule on the matter. The act further established a fine of $500 against any person who aided a fugitive. The act was no doubt a response to the proliferation of anti-slavery societies and to the emergence of the Underground Railroad. Like the Constitution itself, this act does not include a single mention of the words "slave" or "slavery."[5]

With the passage of the Fugitive Slave Act, abolitionists (those who favored ending slavery) now had to deal with laws that would punish any person aiding and abetting slaves in their quest for freedom.

A HOUSE DIVIDED

Despite laws enacted in favor of slave owners, the United States remained divided over the slavery issue, even as the country continued to grow and expand westward. Attempts to curb

UNION AND LIBERTY!   AND   UNION AND SLAVERY!

In the 1864 U.S. presidential election, Democrat George McClellan ran against incumbent and Republican Abraham Lincoln. The Democratic Party largely supported slavery, which is depicted in this broadside where McClellan shakes the hand of Confederate president Jefferson Davis, while a slave auction takes place behind them. On the left, Lincoln shakes hands with a man, while black and white children leave a schoolhouse.

slavery in new territories applying for statehood were met by challenges and countercompromises. Among these were the Missouri Compromise of 1820, the Compromise of 1850, and the Kansas–Nebraska Act of 1854. The passage of each law was an attempt to keep a fine balance between proslavery and anti-slavery supporters, but to no avail. Eventually, a nation divided cannot exist as one, as Abraham Lincoln foreshadowed nearly three years before the outbreak of the Civil War. In his 1858 speech on the eve of his nomination for a U.S. Senate seat for Illinois, Lincoln said:

A house divided against itself cannot stand. I believe this government cannot endure, permanently half *slave* and half *free*. I do not expect the Union to be *dissolved*—I do not expect the house to *fall*—but I *do* expect it will cease to be divided. It will become *all* one thing, or *all* the other. Either the *opponents* of slavery will arrest the further spread of it, and place it where the public mind shall rest in the belief that it is in course of ultimate extinction; or its *advocates* will push it forward, till it shall become alike lawful in *all* the states, *old* as well as *new*—*North* as well as *South*.[6]

Shortly before Lincoln was inaugurated as the sixteenth president of the United States, Southern governors and statesmen called for the proslavery states in the South to secede from the Union. Seven states seceded and formed their own nation, calling it the Confederate States of America. They elected Jefferson Davis as their own president two weeks before Lincoln took his oath of office—with the nation already divided. On April 12, 1861, Confederate troops attacked the Union-held Fort Sumter in South Carolina, one of the states now part of the Confederacy. The conflict led to the escalation of war. Four years later, at the cost of more than 620,000 lives—Union and Confederate—the war ended with the North prevailing. The United States remained a united country. The Civil War forever changed how the federal government would operate, and it marked the end of slavery. And though slavery came to an end with the conclusion of the war, resentment against blacks remained high in the South, resulting in violence, segregation tactics, and outright discrimination against blacks for many, many years to come.

WORKING THROUGH THE LAW

Three amendments to the U.S. Constitution—the Thirteenth, Fourteenth, and Fifteenth—were very important to the civil rights movement. The Thirteenth Amendment, ratified on December 6, 1865, abolished slavery. Section 1 states:

Neither slavery nor involuntary servitude, except as a punishment for crime whereof the party shall have been duly convicted, shall exist within the United States, or any place subject to their jurisdiction."[7] The Fourteenth Amendment, ratified on July 9, 1868, protected the rights of freed slaves: "All persons born or naturalized in the United States, and subject to the jurisdiction thereof, are citizens of the United States and of the State wherein they reside. No State shall make or enforce any law which shall abridge the privileges or immunities of citizens of the United States; nor shall any State deprive any person of life, liberty, or property, without due process of law; nor deny to any person within its jurisdiction the equal protection of the laws."[8] The Fifteenth Amendment, ratified on February 3, 1870, protected blacks' voting rights: "The right of citizens of the United States to vote shall not be denied or abridged by the United States or by any State on account of race, color, or previous condition of servitude.[9]

Voting privileges afforded blacks the opportunity to gain political power, protect their rights, and have an active say in their governance and their own futures. As the country moved into the twentieth century, black integration in society began to emerge. In 1909, Ida Wells-Barnett, W. E. B. Du Bois, Henry Moscowitz, Mary White Ovington, Oswald Garrison Villard, and William English Walling founded the National Association for the Advancement of Colored People, or NAACP. Its mission, as stated in its charter, promises "[to] promote equality of rights and to eradicate caste or race prejudice among the citizens of the United States; to advance the interest of colored citizens; to secure for them impartial suffrage; and to increase their opportunities for securing justice in the courts, education for the children, employment according to their ability and complete equality before law."[10]

Early on in its fight for equality, the NAACP used the courts to try to overturn existing "Jim Crow" (racial discrimination) statutes. Understanding the need to have black legal representation in the court system was the first step in tearing down the walls of racial discrimination and segregation in the country. By confronting the statutes through litigation and lobbying pressure, the NAACP was the most influential organization in winning rights for blacks and equal protection under the law. Little by little, discrimination barriers were being torn down, enabling blacks to fight racial discrimination in a variety of areas, including hiring practices (1941, Executive Order 8802); breaking through the color barrier in sports, with Jackie Robinson becoming the first black to play in the major leagues in 1947; and full integration of the armed services (1948, Executive Order 9981). Each of these victories served as a building block for the full-scale assault on segregation that would begin to take place in the 1950s. The first real test would be the challenge to the "separate but equal" doctrine espoused by the 1896 U.S. Supreme Court decision in *Plessy v. Ferguson*. A victory there could provide the momentum needed to address, by legal means, the wrongful treatment against blacks in many parts of the United States.

Using the
Court of Law

Despite the abolition of slavery in the United States, free blacks still had many rough years of ill treatment in front of them. The major difference was that there were finally some laws that offered legal protection for blacks. Aside from the passage of the Fourteenth Amendment, which guaranteed equal protection under the law for all U.S. citizens, other laws provided blacks with more specific protections. In 1875, the first Civil Rights Act was passed, providing "[that] all persons . . . shall be entitled to full and equal enjoyment of the accommodations, advantages, facilities, and privileges of inns, public conveyances on land or water, theaters, and other places of public amusement."[11] The Supreme Court, however, declared this act unconstitutional in 1883. In their ruling, the court said the act protected social rather than political rights of individuals, and the Fourteenth Amendment "prohibited the states from depriving individuals of their civil rights but did not protect the abuse of individuals' civil rights by other individuals."[12]

The court's ruling ended any federal protection for blacks against discrimination imposed by private persons, opening the door for Southern legislators to write segregation laws. The most notorious means of legally maneuvering to continue keeping blacks segregated was known as "Jim Crow." In *The History of Jim Crow: Creating Jim Crow*, author Ronald L. F. Davis, explains:

> [I]n general the Jim Crow era in American history dates from the late 1890s, when southern states began systematically to codify [strengthen] in law and state constitutional provisions the subordinate position of African Americans in society. Most of these legal steps were aimed at separating the races in public spaces [public schools, parks, accommodations, and transportation] and preventing adult black males from exercising the right to vote. In every state of the former Confederacy, the system of legalized segregation and disfranchisement was fully in place by 1910. This system of white supremacy cut across class boundaries and re-enforced a cult of "whiteness" that predated the Civil War.[13]

PLESSY V. FERGUSON

In 1896, the U.S. Supreme Court handed down a decision that ultimately gave validation to a separate but equal system, which was basically a legal form of segregation. In the minds of many legal scholars, black and white, this doctrine went right to the heart of institutionalized racism in the United States. In the landmark case *Plessy v. Ferguson*, the court upheld the Louisiana Separate Car Law, which required separate but equal railroad car facilities for blacks and whites. To challenge the constitutionality of the law in the state, Homer Plessy, a light-skinned black man, boarded a train and took a seat in the rail car reserved for whites. He was arrested and brought his case to court, arguing that the Louisiana law violated the Thirteenth and Fourteenth amendments to the Constitution. The court ruled against Plessy, stating that Louisiana was free to regulate railroad companies operating within the state. Plessy appealed his case to the Louisiana State Supreme Court, which upheld the lower court's ruling.

With only one appeal left to him, Plessy took his case to the U.S. Supreme Court. The court again upheld the lower courts' rulings. In the majority opinion, Justice Henry Brown wrote:

> That [the Separate Car Act] does not conflict with the Thirteenth Amendment, which abolished slavery . . . is too clear for argument. . . . A statute which implies merely a legal distinction between the white and colored races—a distinction which is founded in the color of the two races, and which must always exist so long as white men are distinguished from the other race by color—has no tendency to destroy the legal equality of the two races. . . . The object of the [Fourteenth Amendment] was undoubtedly to enforce the absolute equality of the two races before the law, but in the nature of things it could not have been intended to abolish distinctions based upon color, or to enforce social, as distinguished from political equality, or a commingling of the two races upon terms unsatisfactory to either.[14]

The lone dissenting judge, Justice John Marshall Harlan, however, wrote that the Constitution of the United States was color blind, and did not distinguish or tolerate classes among its citizens. With regard to civil rights, Harlan wrote that all citizens were equal under the laws of the nation. With incredible insight, Harlan predicted that the court's decision would set a precedent for many other "separate but equal" policies extending into many other areas of public life, including restaurants, theaters, restrooms, water fountains, and even public schools.

Largely influenced by the principles of the Presbyterian Church, Associate Supreme Court Justice John Marshall Harlan was an advocate for civil rights. Harlan, who served on the court for 33 years, cast the lone dissenting vote in the 1896 *Plessy v. Ferguson* case, which upheld racial segregation in the South.

Justice Harlan was right, and *Plessy v. Ferguson* would become *the* case to overturn legalized segregation in the United States.

CHARLES HOUSTON

One year before the *Plessy* decision, a black man was born who would spend most of his adult life trying to eliminate segregation in the United States. That man, Charles Hamilton Houston, spent much of his life living in a segregated society. In some respects, he faired better than other blacks living in Jim Crow America. Residing in the heart of the country's capital city of Washington, D.C., Houston was lucky enough to grow up in a stable home environment. His father was a lawyer and his mother was a hairdresser whose clientele included influential politicians and government officials. His parents provided him with as many advantages as they could afford, taking their son to the zoo, the theater, museums, and concerts. He was also fortunate to attend the M Street High School, the first black high school in the nation. The high school provided a traditional curriculum, instead of the usual trade-school curriculum available to most blacks.

Having done well in high school, he set off for Amherst College, where he was the only black student in his 1915 freshman class. After graduation, Houston returned to Washington, taking a teaching job at Howard University, where he taught English and created the first course in Negro literature. With the outbreak of World War I, Houston enlisted in the army, and attended the black officer's training camp in Des Moines, Iowa. He quickly saw the inequalities between blacks and whites in the military's judicial system. Determined to join a profession in which he could "fight for those who could not strike back," he enrolled at Harvard University Law School. Upon receiving his degree, Houston joined his father's law firm and began teaching law classes at Howard University. In *Eyes on the Prize*, author Juan Williams wrote of Houston's deeply felt conviction that "black people needed black lawyers to represent them . . .

and believed that if the legal system were to change, it would be because of the disciplined and consistent pressure exerted by a cadre of black lawyers."[15]

Howard Law School's facilities were inadequate and there were not enough books to go around. The school also was not allowed to join the state bar association (the regulatory organization for professional lawyers); consequently, Howard students could not use the association's facilities. Houston taught for five years before being named vice dean of the law school. He was then asked to turn the school around. His response to this task was to close down the night school program, impose stricter entrance requirements, and to hire well-respected legal scholars to deliver guest lectures. If Howard University Law School was not going to produce black lawyers equal to their white counterparts, it would not be because they did not have the necessary resources.

Within two years under his direction, the American Bar Association gave Howard Law School full accreditation. Houston never strayed far from his belief that the key to changing discriminatory laws lay in having black lawyers address the inequities in the law. He also believed that the only admirable role for a black lawyer "was that of social engineer—someone who understood the Constitution and knew how to use it to better the living conditions of underprivileged citizens."[16] Houston wanted Howard to produce this kind of lawyer.

LAUNCHING A LEGAL STRATEGY

Houston had long had an affiliation with the NAACP, and often assisted the association with civil rights cases. More than simply an educational institution, Howard provided its students with practical experience working on real cases, researching and preparing material with the possibility that some of those cases could actually end up in court. The legal "soldiers" of the civil rights movement were being amassed. Ironically, it was a white, Harvard-educated lawyer who worked for the

NAACP—Nathan Ross Margold—who was the architect of the legal strategy to bring an end to the separate but equal doctrine. The first line of attack was against the segregation of schools in the United States. Using Margold's strategy, Houston first challenged the segregated professional and graduate schools in the country. He felt that by starting with higher education, where inequities were most glaring, he could build one win upon another, through all levels of education, down to the segregated elementary schools that had become commonplace in the southern states by 1935.

At the time, one of Houston's former Howard students, Thurgood Marshall, was practicing law in Baltimore, Maryland. Marshall told his former professor about a case that involved a black student—Donald Gaines Murray—who was denied admission to the all-white University of Maryland School of Law. Marshall, too, had been rejected by the school due to its preclusion of black students. Together, Houston and Marshall decided to take Murray's case to court to challenge these practices. Appearing before a Baltimore court,

> Marshall argued that Donald Gaines Murray was just as qualified as white applicants to attend the University of Maryland's School of Law and that it was solely due to his race that he was rejected. Furthermore, he argued that since the "black" law schools which Murray would otherwise have to attend were no where near the same academic caliber as the University's law school, the University was violating the principle of "separate but equal." Moreover, Marshall argued that the disparities between the "white" and "black" law schools were so great that the only remedy would be to allow students like Murray to attend the University's law school.[17]

The Baltimore court agreed with Marshall, and though the university took the case to the Maryland State Court of Appeals,

In 1935, Thurgood Marshall (left) and his mentor Charles Houston (right) were instrumental in helping their client Donald G. Murray (center) gain admittance to the University of Maryland School of Law, which at the time only admitted white students. Marshall and Houston argued that because the University of Maryland was a better institution than "black" law schools, the school was violating the principle of "separate but equal," because Murray would not have the same opportunities as white students.

it upheld the lower court's ruling. Murray was permitted to attend the law school and graduated two years after the ruling.

The Murray case was an important victory in the strategy to gain enough legal precedent to challenge the constitutionality of *Plessy v. Ferguson*. "Precedent" is an aspect of the law in which judges use the results of similar cases from the past to decide the outcome of a current case. Throughout 1936, Houston and Marshall (who was now working full time for the NAACP) periodically traveled throughout the South, looking for cases that might serve to challenge segregation practices in the schools. They found one in *Missouri ex rel. Gaines v. Canada*. The case involved 25-year-old Lloyd Lionel Gaines, a black man who was refused admission, despite being qualified, to the University of Missouri School of Law because he was black. Houston headed to Missouri to argue the case on behalf of Gaines, who had appealed a lower level court's decision in favor of the law school. Subsequently, the Missouri Supreme Court upheld the lower court's decision, at which point Houston filed an appeal to the U.S. Supreme Court. It took more than two years for the court to hear the Gaines case, but the inquiry was finally scheduled in early November 1938.

The heart of the case centered around the state of Missouri offering Gaines two options: attending an all-black law school that it would build (at the time, there were no all-black laws schools in Missouri), or having the state assist Gaines financially to attend a law school in a neighboring state. In his argument before the court, Houston stated that denying Gaines admission to the law school violated the Fourteenth Amendment's Equal Protection Clause, effectively saying "the laws of a state must treat an individual in the same manner as others in similar conditions and circumstances."[18] The court agreed. In a 6–2 decision, the U.S. Supreme Court reversed the judgment of the state supreme court, affirming Gaines's right to attend the school. In delivering the opinion of the court, Chief Justice Charles E. Hughes wrote:

> By the operation of the laws of Missouri a privilege has been created for white law students which is denied to Negroes by reason of their race. The white resident is afforded legal education within the State; the Negro resident having the same qualifications is refused it there—and must go outside the

State to obtain it. That is a denial of the equality of legal right to the enjoyment of privilege which the State has set up, and the provision for the payment of tuition fees in another State does not remove that discrimination.[19]

The court's ruling in *Missouri ex rel. Gaines v. Canada* had broad implications on future discrimination cases. Based on the finding that states would now be required to provide an equal law school (or other level of) education to its black citizens, would they also have to provide equal-education opportunities in their undergraduate institutions? Would the ruling also include high schools? Middle schools? Elementary schools? Had Houston's strategy to attack segregation by first challenging the educational system been right after all? And could the judgment in *Missouri ex rel. Gaines v. Canada* also be applied to other public establishments like theaters, restaurants, parks, and hospitals?

THE ROAD TO *BROWN V. BOARD OF EDUCATION*
In 1940, the NAACP created the Legal Defense and Educational Fund, Inc. (LDF), the first organization of its kind that worked within the court system to "secure equal justice under the law for all individuals." Thurgood Marshall wrote the code of practice for it and was named the LDF's first director counsel.

Throughout the 1940s, several discrimination cases, some having nothing to do with the educational system, made their way through the courts, ending in judgments that further eroded the separate but equal practices in the country. In *Alston v. School Board of City of Norfolk* (1940), a case involving pay discrimination, a court ordered the school board to pay black teachers a salary equal to that of their white colleagues. In the Texas case of *Smith v. Allwright* (1944), one that addressed voting rights, the U.S. Supreme Court ruled 8–1 that a law excluding blacks from voting in the state's Democratic primary elections violated the Fifteenth Amendment. The victories for Marshall and the LDF had enormous significance. It was a huge blow to existing Jim Crow segregation practices. Moreover, as author Charles L. Zelden has written:

> [I]t provided the conceptual foundation which underlay Thurgood Marshall's successful arguments in *Brown v. Board of Education* . . . the *Smith* decision attacked the intractable heart of segregation, as it redrew the boundary between public and private action in constitutional law and laid the groundwork for many civil rights cases to come.[20]

With these cases behind him, Marshall took on two cases that would attack the separate but equal doctrine itself. In the first case, Herman Sweatt, a black mailman who had applied for admission to the law school at the University of Texas in Austin, was told that the school would set up a program for him in the basement of a small building and provide part-time faculty for his instruction. The other case involved a 68-year-old professor named G. W. McLaurin. Initially denied entrance to a Ph.D. program at the University of Oklahoma, McLaurin was later provided a desk surrounded by a railing with a sign that read "reserved for colored." He was also required to eat at a separate table in the school's cafeteria, as well as study at a separate table in the library.

The U.S. Supreme Court heard arguments by Marshall for both the *Sweatt* and *McLaurin* cases on the same day. Marshall argued that Sweatt was not being afforded the same legal education that the university was providing its white students. In the case of McLaurin, Marshall stated that although the Ph.D. candidate was permitted to attend the same classes, eat the same food, and have access to the same resources at the library as his white counterparts, he was being denied an equal education due to the restrictions and segregation he had to endure.

Marshall and his legal team had to wait more than a month for the court to render its opinions. In the meantime, the man behind the legal strategy of challenging *Plessy v. Ferguson*, Charles Houston, died. His 20-year dedication to bringing an

THURGOOD MARSHALL
(1908–1993)

First African-American
Supreme Court Justice

One of the greatest advocates of civil rights, Thurgood Marshall gained recognition early in his legal career. While chief legal counsel for the NAACP, he successfully argued more than 30 cases in front of the U.S. Supreme Court, focusing his efforts on civil rights cases aimed at overturning *Plessy v. Ferguson*. Marshall's greatest victory, *Brown v. Board of Education*, forever changed the landscape of racial segregation across the nation. The court's unanimous decision brought an end to the practice of segregation in public schools and set a movement in motion that continues to this day.

Despite opposition by some southern senators in 1961, Marshall became a justice on the U.S. Court of Appeals Second Circuit through an appointment by President John F. Kennedy. The Senate confirmed Marshall on September 11, 1962. He served on the appeals court until appointed by President Lyndon Johnson to the U.S. Supreme Court on June 13, 1967. Marshall's confirmation was a historic one, because he had become the first African American to sit on the high court. As an associate justice, Marshall was a proponent of affirmative action and never wavered in his fight for equality for all under the law.

In his later years on the court, Marshall felt isolated, finding himself surrounded by a more conservative group of justices. The onset of ill health and a growing disillusionment prompted Marshall to retire in 1991. The very conservative and very controversial Clarence Thomas replaced him on the bench.

end to "separate but equal" received a boost when on June 5 the Supreme Court rendered its decision. The court, writing an opinion that narrowly defined their majority ruling, did agree that separate but equal had to be just that or the separation, in whatever form, was unconstitutional.

LANDMARK DECISION RENDERED

The case that would become the lightning rod for the civil rights movement originated in America's heartland—Topeka, Kansas. A seven-year-old girl named Linda Brown would soon be immortalized in civil rights history. Brown's father, Oliver, the catalyst for the lawsuit, sought the assistance of the NAACP in challenging segregation in his hometown. As Linda explained years later, "My father pondered 'Why? Why should my child walk four miles when there is a school only four blocks away?' He wondered 'Why should I take time to explain to my daughter that she can't attend school with her neighborhood playmates because she is black?'"[21] The irony was that since 1941, after a local court ordered the integration of public schools from the junior high level through high school, black and white students had been attending school together. The *Brown* case would offer an excellent opportunity to question the legality of legalized segregation in Topeka, and by extension, the nation.

The case is widely known as *Brown v. Board of Education*, but was in actuality a grouping of five cases, all concerning the issues of segregation in public schools. The cases—*Briggs et al. v. Elliott et al.* (Clarendon County, South Carolina), *Davis v. the School Board of Prince Edward County* (Farmville, Virginia), *Bulah v. Gebhart* (New Castle, Delaware), *Bolling v. Sharpe* (Washington, D.C.), and *Brown et al. v. the Board of Education of Topeka, Kansas*—were all heard by the U.S. Supreme Court during its October term in 1952. The cases were consolidated under the name of the first case the court decided to hear—*Brown v. the Board of Education of Topeka, Kansas*—for a very specific reason. Associate Justice Tom Clark explained why: "We felt it was much better to have

In 1951, Oliver Brown brought a class-action suit against the Topeka, Kansas, Board of Education, because it would not allow his daughter Linda (pictured here) to attend an elementary school in her neighborhood. The case was eventually brought before the U.S. Supreme Court, which ruled in *Brown v. Board of Education* that racial segregation was no longer applicable in the public school system.

representative cases from different parts of the country, so we consolidated them and made Brown the first so that the whole question would not smack of being a purely Southern one."[22]

Marshall and the LDF had been working toward this opportunity for the last 12 years. Marshall presented arguments to the court on behalf of the plaintiffs, or the parties who brought the lawsuits to court. There was a good deal at stake. If the court overturned the lower courts' rulings, 50 years of adherence to the separate but equal doctrine, and all the cases, including the *Plessy v. Ferguson* ruling, would be swept away. A victory would effectively outlaw racial segregation. After hearing arguments for six days from attorneys on both sides of the issue, the Supreme Court justices convened to consider their decision. However, after nine months of reviewing the evidence, the court had still not issued a ruling. The ruling was further postponed when Chief Justice Fred Vinson died and the makeup of the court suddenly changed.

To replace Vinson on the court, President Dwight Eisenhower appointed California governor Earl Warren. Based on his past positions, Warren was a question mark in the minds of the NAACP. He had taken strong stands in favor of equality for all citizens, and was an advocate for fair employment practices. However, Warren also strongly supported the U.S. government's disgraceful policy of imprisoning Japanese Americans during World War II. The opponents of segregation did not need to worry, though, as Warren was able to do what Vinson had not—end the deadlock between the other justices and gain a unanimous decision. It has been written that Warren struck a deal with Justice Stanley Reed, who had wanted to write a dissenting opinion. The two agreed that if Reed voted with the majority, giving Warren his unanimous decision, Warren would agree to permit the gradual dismantling of segregation, rather than ordering its immediate implementation.

On Monday, May 17, 1954, more than one and a half years after the first arguments were heard in *Brown v. Board*

As a result of the 1954 *Brown v. Board of Education* decision, schools throughout the United States were integrated. Pictured here is a group of second and third graders who are waiting to receive supplies during the first day of school at an elementary school in Springer, Oklahoma, in 1958.

of Education, the Warren court delivered its opinion. Its significance cannot be overstated. In the unanimous opinion, Warren wrote:

These cases come to us from the States of Kansas, South Carolina, Virginia, and Delaware. They are premised on different facts and different local conditions, but a common legal question justifies their consideration together in this consolidated opinion. . . . In approaching this problem, we cannot turn the clock back to 1868 when the Amendment was adopted, or even to 1896 when *Plessy v. Ferguson* was written. We must consider public education in the light of its full development and its present place in American life throughout the Nation. Only in this way can it be determined if segregation in public schools deprives these plaintiffs of the equal protection of the laws. . . . We come then to the question presented: Does segregation of children in public schools solely on the basis of race, even though the physical facilities and other "tangible" factors may be equal, deprive the children of the minority group of equal educational opportunities? We believe that it does. . . . We conclude that in the field of public education the doctrine of "separate but equal" has no place.[23]

The court's decision set off a firestorm of protest and resistance, but more importantly, as an editorial in the May 19, 1954, edition of the *Washington Post* said, "It is not too much to speak of the Court's decision as a new birth of freedom. It comes at a juncture in the affairs of mankind when this reaffirmation of basic human values is likely to have a wonderfully tonic effect."[24] Somewhere, in spirit, Charles Houston was celebrating with the lawyers he had so skillfully trained to take on this monumental task.

Getting America's Attention

M ay 17, 1954, became known in the South as Black Monday, the day the U.S. Supreme Court handed down its decision in *Brown v. Board of Education*, striking down the separate but equal doctrine set forth by the *Plessy v. Ferguson* decision almost 50 years earlier. The *Plessy* decision had given southern segregationist state legislators free reign to enact laws that imposed different policies for blacks in virtually every aspect of life—from where they could eat, ride a train, go to school, and even vote. The *Brown* ruling had an indelible impact on blacks and whites, forever changing treatment endured and unconscionable treatment gone unchecked for so long. "The 1954 decision shook the entire world socially, politically, and economically, laid the foundation for new civil rights laws, policies and practices, and prompted civil rights struggles around the globe . . ."[25]

The court failed to provide any guidelines on how those affected by the ruling should begin implementing the desegregation of their schools. But this was a fact almost lost amid the fiery anger and rage the decision provoked from southern politicians and many of their citizens. In no place was this more apparent than in Mississippi. At the time, Mississippi was perhaps the most racially discriminatory state in the nation, and it was not a safe place to be shortly after May 17, 1954, if you were black, or if you were white and vocally supportive of desegregation. Fed by deeply rooted anger and rage over the court's decision, some whites took their fury to the streets, vandalizing property and randomly attacking, savagely beating, and even hanging innocent blacks throughout the state.

A more subtle but effective means of harassing blacks also became prevalent, by way of economic intimidation. Known simply as the White Citizens' Council, members were recruited from all professions—bankers, plantation owners, physicians, lawyers, business owners, even members of the clergy. The idea behind establishing the council was to make it nearly impossible for any black advocating desegregation to obtain or hold onto a job, establish a good financial record, acquire a mortgage to buy a home, receive medical treatment, or any number of other activities that come up in the course of day-to-day living. The council met openly, and very little stigma was attached to being a member. Unlike the Ku Klux Klan, the council did not advocate violence. It quickly spread beyond Mississippi to other parts of the South, effectively imposing economic pressure on blacks for several years after the *Brown* decision.

RACIAL INJUSTICE MOUNTS

It was not unheard of in the 1950s to learn that a seemingly innocent black person had been murdered in the racially charged towns and cities of the Deep South. With little or no provocation, white hate groups randomly went after blacks. Even the appearance of not showing proper respect for a white person in his or her presence often brought brutal retaliation, and rarely were the perpetrators punished. It was not uncommon for a black child to be assaulted simply for not stepping aside on the sidewalk to let a white person walk by. In particular, two murders that occurred in Mississippi in 1955 were not random, and were intended to invoke fear and intimidation to "nigras" who were considered to be stirring up other "nigras" and needed to be reminded of their place.

The first victim, Reverend George W. Lee, had grown up poor like many blacks of his time in Mississippi. Determined to make something of his life, Lee graduated from high school and later accepted a position as a preacher in Belzoni, Mississippi, a predominantly poor, black community. Soon Lee was running four churches and a local grocery store. He and his wife, Rosebud, even set up a small printing business in the back of the store. Wanting to help his poor black church members, Lee began to plant the seeds of a civil rights movement in his hometown. He became the first black man in all of Humphreys County in memory to register to vote. With the help of friend Gus Courts, Lee established a local branch of the NAACP, and the two campaigned to register as many blacks to vote as possible. This did not sit well with white supremacists in Mississippi.

During the course of time, because of Lee's voter-registration campaigns and participation in other desegregation activities, he made enemies—angry enemies. He received threatening notes and visits from men. To shield her from the threats against him, Lee told his wife the "visitors" were just salesmen. One evening, though, the threats were acted upon. While Lee was driving home, a car pulled alongside him and an unidentified assailant fired three shotgun blasts at him, hitting him in the face. Lee swerved off the road, crashed his car, and died. The local sheriff and coroner tried to attribute Lee's death to the crash, but an autopsy revealed several shotgun pellets in his face. Lee's funeral captured the attention of every black news organization in the nation, which in turn reported the story throughout the United States. Lee's murderers were never found and brought to justice. His death exemplified to an otherwise passive country the racial injustice and violence against blacks in the South who dared to stand up for their rights.

A few months after Lee's murder, a 14-year-old black Chicago native visiting relatives in Money, Mississippi, was roused from sleep and taken from his relatives' house in the middle of the night. Three days later, the body of that boy, Emmett Till, was pulled from the Tallahatchie River. He had been brutally beaten and shot in the head. Emmett had made the trip from Chicago with his cousin Wheeler Parker. The two boys had been staying with their great-uncle, Moses Wright, a cotton sharecropper and preacher who had lived in the Delta area for a long time. Described as a smart dresser, a practical jokester, and rather grown-up looking for his age, Emmett was hanging out outside Bryant's Grocery and Meat Store with Wheeler and several other cousins and friends one balmy evening in August. He allegedly boasted about having a white girlfriend back in Chicago, and was goaded by one of the other boys to go inside the store and talk to one of the white women behind the counter. Soon after, Emmett came out of the store and allegedly said "Bye, baby" to the woman.

The woman to whom he was speaking was Carolyn Bryant, the wife of the store's owner. She came out right behind Emmett, threatening to get her pistol and shoot him. As Emmett and Wheeler jumped into their great-uncle's car, Emmett "wolf whistled" at Bryant as they sped off. Even though she decided not to tell her husband, Roy, what happened, news of the incident spread around town. Some folks warned Emmett that when Roy Bryant found out, there was going to be trouble. Three days later, there was. Roy Bryant and his half brother J. W. Milam found out where Emmett was staying, and arrived at Moses Wright's cabin at 2:00 A.M. armed with pistols to get the boy who had disrespected his wife. Despite Wright's pleas on behalf of his great-nephew, Bryant

In 1955, Chicago resident Emmett Till was brutally murdered in Mississippi in retaliation for allegedly whistling at a white woman. The two suspects in the murder, Roy Bryant and J. W. Milam, were acquitted, despite overwhelming evidence supporting their guilt.

and Milam dragged Emmett out of the cabin, put him into Bryant's car, and sped off.

Emmett was so badly beaten that his great-uncle was only able to identify him by an initial ring on his nephew's finger. When his body arrived in Chicago for burial, Mamie Till-Bradley insisted on an open-casket funeral so the world could see what had been done to her son. The image of Emmett in his coffin began to circulate in black newspapers and magazines throughout the United States. The sight of the boy's body and the savagery by which he had been murdered sickened and angered black America in a way not even segregation had. Cries for justice and "criticism of the barbarity of segregation" in Mississippi only galvanized the South's reaction.

Bryant and Milam were arrested and charged with kidnapping even before Emmett's body was found. Initially, no local white attorney would represent them. But criticism from northerners rankled whites in Mississippi, and soon Bryant and Milam had all the support they needed. Only a few weeks after Emmett was buried, Bryant and Milam were brought to trial. Despite death threats, Moses Wright bravely took the stand to testify in front of an all-white, male jury in a segregated courthouse in Sumner, Mississippi, in mid-September 1955. Asked by the prosecution if he could identify the men who had come to his cabin and taken away his nephew, Wright pointed to Milam and then Bryant. Others bravely testified, as well, including field hand Willie Reed, who told the court he had seen Bryant, Milam, a few other white men, and three blacks, including Emmett, racing down a dirt road toward Milam's brother's plantation. Hearing screams from the barn a short while later, Reed testified that he walked closer to the barn to see what was going on, only to be met by a pistol-carrying Milam. Scared, Reed told Milam he saw nothing and quickly left.

The courage of those who stood in fear of white reprisals was in vain. In closing arguments, John C. Whitten, counsel for

Bryant and Milam, said to the jury, "Your fathers will turn over in their graves if [Milam and Bryant are found guilty] and I'm sure that every last Anglo-Saxon one of you has the courage to free these men in the face of that [outside] pressure."[26] After deliberating for a little more than an hour, the jury returned their verdict: not guilty. Later, jury foreman J. W. Shaw was overheard justifying the verdict as a failure of the state to prove the body was that of Emmett Till.

Reaction to the verdict from black *and* white America was one of outrage and disgust with the justice system in Mississippi. Prominent blacks organized protest rallies in major cities throughout the country. NAACP executive director Roy Wilkins told a crowd in Harlem, New York, "It would appear from this lynching that the State of Mississippi has decided to maintain white supremacy by murdering children. The killers of the boy felt free to lynch him because there is in the entire state no restraining influence of decency, not in the state capital, among the daily newspapers, the clergy nor any segment of the so-called better citizens."[27]

In the cruelest of ironies in the justice system, Bryant and Milam admitted to killing Emmett in an interview with *Look* magazine editor William Bradford Huie. The article was published in the January 1956 issue. Under the "double jeopardy" rule of law, a person cannot be tried twice for the same offense, and so even though they confessed, Bryant and Milam literally got away with murder. It was an awakening to blacks everywhere. Mamie Till-Bradley may have expressed it best when she said, "Two months ago I had a nice apartment in Chicago. I had a good job. I had a son. When something happened to the Negroes in the South I said, 'That's their business, not mine.' Now I know how wrong I was. The murder of my son has shown me that what happens to any of us, anywhere in the world, had better be the business of us all."[28]

ENDURING JIM CROW

The incidents of violence against blacks, such as the murders of George W. Lee and Emmett Till, were certainly at the extreme end of what blacks in the South had to endure under Jim Crow society. Lynchings, beatings, and destruction of property left blacks in a constant state of fear. As a housekeeper for a white family at the time of the Emmett Till murder and trial, civil rights activist Anne Moody recalled what went through her own mind as a black living in a white-supremacist state:

> Before Emmett Till's murder, I had known the fear of hunger, hell, and the Devil. But now there was a new fear known to me—the fear of being killed just because I was black. This was the worst of my fears. I knew once I got food, the fear of starving to death would leave. I also was told that if I were a good girl, I wouldn't have to fear the Devil or hell. But I didn't know what one had to do or not do as a Negro not to be killed. Probably just being a Negro period was enough, I thought.[29]

If you were black and living in the South, there were indignities to endure that were part of everyday life, because racial discrimination went beyond public school segregation. Water fountains were designated "For Whites Only" or "For Colored Only." Restaurants, theaters, restrooms, stores, buses, trains, and other public facilities were delineated based on whether you were white or black. Even walking down the street required deference to a passing white person. Defiance of these Jim Crow laws only brought more pain and misery to an otherwise difficult life.

Society was changing, though. Taking their cue from other courageous blacks like Moses Wright and Mamie Till-Bradley, blacks in Montgomery, Alabama, were going to challenge the daily indignity thrust upon them by traveling on segregated buses in the city.

During the era of Jim Crow laws—1877 through the 1950s—southern blacks were forced to endure racial segregation. In addition to attending their own schools, blacks were not permitted to use many public facilities. Oftentimes, they had to use their own facilities, such as the water fountain pictured here in Halifax, North Carolina.

Segregated city buses were the norm in the South. But it went even further than the humiliation and discomfort that resulted in adhering to the division that existed between sitting sections for whites and blacks. White passengers entered the front of the bus, paid their fare, and always had a seat on the bus as long as other whites did not take up all the seats. Upon paying the fare at the front of the bus, black passengers—40,000 daily riders versus 12,000 white riders—had to exit and reenter using the rear bus door. Black passengers were only allowed to sit in the area of the bus designated for blacks, which was in the rear section. And although not legally required to give up a seat to a white person if the white section was full, Montgomery City Line bus drivers regularly ordered blacks to move farther back, redesignating the area for whites only. Often, black passengers would still have to stand while seats in the white section emptied.

After Jo Ann Robinson, an Alabama State College English professor and later president of the Women's Political Council, had been humiliated by a bus driver after she accidentally sat in the front section of a nearly empty bus, she decided to do something about it. After receiving few concessions from the bus company (they agreed to stop at every corner in black neighborhoods just as they did in white ones), Robinson wrote to the mayor, W. A. Gayle, advising him that if blacks did not use the buses, they could not continue to operate on white patronage alone. A successful bus boycott in 1953 by the black residents of Baton Rouge, Louisiana, provided the inducement for a possible boycott in Montgomery. Robinson and the Women's Political Council put together a plan to execute such a boycott, waiting for the right moment to set it in motion.

"YOU MAY DO THAT"

Rosa Parks, 43, a seamstress by trade and secretary of the Montgomery chapter of the NAACP, was no stranger to the indignities of racial segregation. As a young woman of 32, she had suffered the humiliation of being thrown off a Montgomery bus for refusing to reenter through the rear door after paying her fare. The bus driver, James F. Blake, had kept her fare, told her to get off the bus, and driven off.

When Robinson began setting the stage for change in Montgomery, Parks, along with civil rights leader E. D. Nixon and the NAACP, started to prepare a case to take to federal court. The case involved Blake, the same driver Parks had encountered years earlier. Blake had recently had a pregnant 15-year-old girl named Claudette Colvin dragged off his bus and arrested for refusing to give up her seat. Unfortunately, Nixon felt Colvin's unwed pregnancy would attract the wrong kind of press and would harm their case. Nixon felt they needed someone beyond personal reproach. With the Christmas season approaching, Nixon received an early gift.

Parks had been working part time as a seamstress and tailor's assistant at the Montgomery Fair Department Store. At 5:30 P.M. on Thursday, December 1, Parks boarded a bus to go home, and took a seat directly behind the white section. At the next stop, several whites got on the bus, filling up the rest of the whites-only seating area. One white man was left without a seat. Parks was sitting in a row with three other black passengers. Because rules dictated that a black person could not sit in the same row as a white person, all four of them would have to move back for the one white man. Ironically, the bus driver that evening was again Blake. According to Parks, Blake said, "All right, you folks, I want those two seats! Y'all better make it light on yourselves and let me have those seats!"[30] The other passengers moved, but Parks refused. Blake then told Parks that he would have to call the police and have her arrested. She replied, "You may do that."[31] Shortly after, a patrol car arrived where Blake had parked the bus to wait for the officers. Two policemen boarded the bus, asked Parks if she was refusing to give up her seat, upon which she replied, "Yes." They escorted Parks off the bus and took her downtown, fingerprinted her, and booked her for violating the bus segregation ordinance.

THE BUS BOYCOTT BEGINS

After posting her bail, Nixon told Parks that he had a proposition for her—he wondered if she would let him use her case to try to break the bus segregation laws in Montgomery. Parks agreed to let Nixon use her case for the greater cause, despite

ROSA PARKS
(1913–2005)

The "Mother of the Modern Civil Rights Movement"

Rosa Parks's quiet act of defiance during an otherwise uneventful December day in 1955 was part of the beginning of the end to racial segregation in the United States. Refusing to give up her seat near the front of the bus to a white passenger, Parks became a figurehead for a movement that captured the attention of the nation.

She was born on February 4, 1913, in Tuskegee, Alabama, to James and Leona McCauley. Raised and educated in a segregated environment, Parks learned early on to take advantage of opportunities that presented themselves. She understood just how infrequent those opportunities were. "Back then, we didn't have any civil rights. It was just a matter of survival, of existing from one day to the next,"* she said in an interview years later.

After receiving her formal education at the Alabama State Teachers College, Parks settled into life in Montgomery with her husband, Raymond, and worked as a seamstress and housekeeper. Both wanting to work toward improving the quality of life for blacks in the South, Parks and her husband joined the local chapter of the NAACP. In 1943, Parks was elected secretary of the association. She had also been quietly protesting segregation in her own way, taking the stairs in a building rather than riding on an elevator designated "colored only" and going thirsty rather than drinking from a "colored only" water fountain; she would even walk home from work rather than be forced to sit in the back of the bus. Parks put it best when she said, "Differences of race, nationality, or religion should not be used to deny any human being citizenship rights or privileges."** Parks took advantage of an opportunity on that winter day in 1955 and helped change the lives of countless others.

---

* Academy of Achievement, "Rosa Parks." Available online at
   www.achievement.org/autodoc/page/par0bio-1
** Ibid.

On December 1, 1955, Rosa Parks was arrested and fined $10 for violating Montgomery, Alabama's segregation ordinance for city buses after she refused to give up her seat to a white passenger. Civil Rights activist Edgar Daniel Nixon (center), pictured here with Parks and attorney Fred Gray, was instrumental in convincing Parks to challenge Montgomery's disriminatory seating policy.

the potential danger it might bring to her and her family. Nixon contacted several black ministers in Montgomery, including Ralph Abernathy, minister of the First Baptist Church. They agreed to meet that Friday evening to discuss strategy.

Upon learning of Parks's arrest, Jo Ann Robinson contacted the other members at the Women's Political Council. They urged Robinson to use Parks's day in court, scheduled for that Monday, as the day to initiate a citywide bus boycott. Robinson prepared and had a handbill distributed explaining what had happened and requesting that all blacks refrain from riding the buses on December 5 to protest the arrest and trial of Rosa Parks. Nixon also got the word out, calling *Montgomery Advertiser* reporter Joe Azbell. He provided him with the leaflet, explaining that the black community was tired of the bus company's treatment of black women. Azbell ran with the story and it appeared on the front page of the *Advertiser*.

News of the planned boycott had spread, but many of the organizers wondered if blacks would unite under this cause and stay off the buses. A young black minister of the Dexter Avenue Baptist Church, Martin Luther King Jr., and his wife, Coretta, rose on Monday morning to the same uncertainty. However, when the first bus passed by their home, Coretta King cried with joy. It was empty. They knew then that the boycott would be a success because the bus that went past their house normally transported more blacks than any other line in the city.

While the boycott unfolded on Montgomery's streets, Parks was found guilty of violating the segregation ordinance and fined $10, plus $4 in court fees. That night, Abernathy and the other black leaders and organizers met and decided to form the Montgomery Improvement Association (MIA). King, noted for his tremendous oratory skills, was elected president. The group debated the merits and drawbacks of continuing the boycott beyond that one day. Some felt it would not last a week. The group decided to take a vote at a meeting that night and let the people of Montgomery decide.

No one knew how many people would actually come to the meeting. They had no need to worry, though, because people packed the Holt Street Baptist Church. King, only 26 years old, rose to give the most important speech of his young life and perhaps of the civil rights movement itself. To an already excited crowd, King said:

> There comes a time that people get tired. We are here this evening to say to those who have mistreated us so long that we are tired—tired of being segregated and humiliated; tired of being kicked about by the brutal feet of oppression. . . . For many years we have shown amazing patience. We have sometimes given our white brothers the feeling that we like the way we are being treated. But we come here tonight to be saved from that patience that makes us patient with anything less than freedom and justice. One of the great glories of democracy is the right to protest for right. . . . If you will protest courageously and yet with dignity and Christian love, when the history books are written in future generations the historians will pause and say, "There lived a great people, a black people who injected new meaning and dignity into the veins of civilization." That is our challenge and our overwhelming responsibility.[32]

STRENGTH IN UNITY

The MIA was not looking to end segregation on the buses; they would leave that to the courts. Their demands only included courteous treatment, first-come, first-served seating with whites still seated in the front of the bus and blacks seated in the back, and the hiring of black drivers on the lines that drove on the black bus routes.

The city commissioners rejected these moderate requests. King realized that merely requesting changes within the segregation laws would not work. The people in power would never agree. The complete end to segregation would be the only way blacks would change the injustice and equality of the current system. As the boycott continued, the city commissioners tried to break it through fines, intimidation, and even falsely advertising in the newspaper that the boycott had ended. Blacks dug in, adamant that now was the time to take a stand. They endured inconveniences, bad weather, harassment, fear of reprisals by hate groups, even the threat of losing their jobs.

Montgomery's blacks remained united even after the violence began. King's house was bombed on January 30, 1956, and a month later, Nixon's house was, too. On February 21, a grand jury indicted King and 24 other ministers for conspiring to boycott. By this time, it was a national story of huge proportion. Lines were being drawn. In March, nearly 100 southern congressmen signed what was known as the Southern Manifesto, in protest of the Supreme Court's *Brown* decision. Lyndon Johnson (who would later preside over another historic civil rights victory), Estes Kefauver, and Albert Gore Sr., were the only southern congressmen who refused to sign.

While King and others worked to maintain unity, civil rights lawyer Fred Gray was busy challenging the segregation issue in the court of law. Representing five women who were challenging the constitutional legality of bus segregation, Gray filed a lawsuit, *Browder v. Gayle*, in federal court on their behalf. The women won the suit, but the city commissioners appealed the case to the U.S. Supreme Court. On November 13, 1956, the court handed down its decision, a ruling that was a blow to segregationists. The Supreme Court affirmed the lower court's ruling, declaring segregation practices on buses unconstitutional.

It took another month before the Supreme Court's written mandate arrived in Montgomery, officially ending bus segregation. The next day, after successfully boycotting the Montgomery City Line bus company for 381 days, black passengers were once again riding the buses in Montgomery. The end of the bus boycott, however, was by no means the end to the fledgling civil rights movement. King and others would now take the cause on to the next level.

The Movement Gains Momentum

News of what happened with the Montgomery bus boycott quickly spread to other cities throughout the South. Blacks became united and drew strength from church organizations, civic leaders, civil rights activists, and others intent on continuing a movement toward the rightful equality and justice they deserved. The bus boycott had been the signal to blacks throughout the United States that a new chapter in the struggle for equality had begun. Leaders of the modern civil rights movement included King, Abernathy, Reverend C. K. Steele, and Reverend T. J. Jemison.

A young and energized King wanted to carry over the success of the Alabama bus boycott to bring an end to racial discrimination and inequality in other areas of life—segregated lunch-counter cafes at department stores, water fountains, theaters, restrooms, and discrimination in employment practices.

He was committed to mobilizing these challenges to Jim Crow in a nonviolent way. Explaining his belief for promoting a non-violent approach to social change, King said, "Non-violence is a powerful and just weapon which cuts without wounding and ennobles the man who wields it."[33] King would earn an extraordinary place in the chronicles of world history, not so much because he became the leader of a cause, but more as a result of the way in which he led it.

Back in Montgomery, 60 ministers from 10 southern states met with King, the unofficial "ordained" leader of the civil rights cause, to discuss how to take the success of the bus boycott and incorporate it into a much larger plan of action. The first step in that process was the creation of a formal organization to represent the civil rights movement. They called the organization the Southern Christian Leadership Conference (SCLC). King and the leadership of the SCLC had bigger plans, ones that involved more than just having blacks gain the right to sit anywhere they chose on a public bus. They wanted to work toward breaking down the walls of segregation, even if it meant pulling the stones out one by one, to create a nation where all people—black and white, male and female, young and old—were "One Nation under God, indivisible, with liberty and justice for all."

GAINS MADE ARE NOT ENOUGH

By the end of the 1950s, blacks had made strides in breaking the "chains" of Jim Crow laws. The *Brown* ruling, the Montgomery bus boycott, even passage of the first Civil Rights Act in 1957 (primarily aimed at securing the right to vote for blacks)—these historic events were a start on the road to ending racism in the United States. But there was so much more to undo; practices that had been long accepted and permitted to exist would need to be met head-on if change was going to occur.

A key to change was in educating blacks on how to participate in the struggle for equality. Teaching nonviolent methods to reject segregationist practices was a main part of that. Pamphlets and flyers were written and distributed. Workshops were organized. Methods taught included sit-ins, organized marches, strikes, boycotts, voter-registration drives—all non-violent means of protest. King had learned these methods from members of the Fellowship of Reconciliation (FOR), an organization that dates back to the early part of the twentieth century. Their vision has been to "carry on programs and educational projects concerned with domestic and international peace and justice, nonviolent alternatives to conflict, and the rights of conscience. A Nonviolent, Interfaith, tax-exempt organization, the FOR promotes nonviolence and has members from many religious and ethnic traditions."[34]

FROM PEACEFUL TO VIOLENT

The plan was to focus on one area of segregation at a time. One of the first places at which King and others wanted to test some of the workshop strategies was at store lunch counters. Department-store and neighborhood luncheonettes routinely refused to serve food or drink to any black customers. The plan was to send several black volunteers to luncheonettes to sit down and wait for service. They would continue to sit until the store closed or until they were served. It was hoped that it would act like a domino effect—once one lunch establishment was integrated, blacks would patronize another establishment until that, too, was integrated. After all the restaurants were integrated, blacks would move on to the next type of segregated business or service—movie theaters, restrooms, water fountains—anyplace that practiced segregation would be targeted. Businesses nationwide would feel the impact from boycotts, because blacks would begin to refuse to patronize department stores that were segregated.

The first known challenge to the whites-only lunch-counter service occurred on February 1, 1960, in Greensboro, North Carolina. Four college freshmen at the all-black North Carolina

On February 1, 1960, four black students sat down at a segregated lunch counter at a F. W. Woolworth store in Greensboro, North Carolina, but were refused service. In response, students throughout the country began to boycott Woolworth stores and organized sit-in protests, including here, where City College of New York students sit at a lunch counter at a Woolworth store in Herald Square.

Agricultural and Technical College—Franklin McCain, Joseph McNeil, Ezell Blair Jr., and David Richmond—walked into a Woolworth's Department Store in downtown Greensboro. The store was open to both whites and blacks, but the restaurant was only open to whites. After purchasing a few items in the store, all four took seats at the lunch counter and tried to order coffee. The white waitress told McCain and his friends that the restaurant did not serve blacks. The students remained at the counter, without being served, until the store closed. The four realized they would need help with this strategy, and they got it from Congress of Racial Equality (CORE) representative Gordon Carey. The new strategy would be to engage in further sit-ins, targeting specific department-store lunch counters—Woolworth's and S. H. Kress—and to mobilize as many students as were necessary to continue the sit-ins on a daily basis.

Soon, Carey and others were implementing the sit-in strategy in other cities. Day after day, the sit-ins grew, drawing more and more participants. News reports carried stories of sit-ins in a host of cities and towns, in both the North and South, from Tallahassee, Florida, and Rock Hill, South Carolina, to High Point, North Carolina, and New York City. White students joined black students at these sit-ins to demonstrate to all Americans that, as Columbia University student Martin Smolin said, ". . . [I]njustice anywhere is everybody's concern."[35]

At first, reactions to the sit-ins were nonviolent. In some cases, store owners reacted by hanging signs that stated: "Closed—In the interest of Public Safety," to "No Trespassing—We reserve the right to serve the public as we see fit." However, protests took a decidedly violent turn on February 27, 1960. During a lunch-counter sit-in at a Nashville, Tennessee, department-store restaurant, dozens of black students were attacked by a group of white teens. Several of the black students were pulled off the counter stools and beaten. When the police arrived, they did not arrest a single

DIANE NASH
(1938–)

Founding Member of the Student Nonviolent Coordinating Committee

A founding member of the Student Nonviolent Coordinating Committee (SNCC), Diane Nash was a vital figure in the American civil rights movement. Having grown up in a middle-class Catholic family on the south side of Chicago, Nash knew little of the Jim Crow racial segregation in the southern states. It was not until she transferred to Fisk University in Nashville, Tennessee, in 1959 that she felt an emotional response to the treatment of blacks. Signs of "For Colored Only" or "Whites Only Served Here" outraged the young student so much that she looked to connect with those who were trying to undo Jim Crow.

Nash's search led her to Reverend James Lawson's nonviolent civil disobedience workshops. Though she learned much from Lawson's classes, Nash was just 22 and wondered what change she could bring about when segregation policy was controlled by governors, judges, local elected officials, and merchants. Emboldened by students demonstrating in other cities throughout the South, Nash became one of the movement's young people who affected change nonviolently—participating in lunch-counter sit-ins and advocating, but not posting, bail money after an arrest. After one arrest, Nash spoke on behalf of all those charged, explaining to the judge, "We feel that if we pay these fines we would be contributing to and supporting the injustice and immoral practices that have been performed in the arrest and conviction of the defendants."[*]

Nash may have helped escalate the desegregation of Nashville's lunch counters when she got Mayor Ben West to agree that it was wrong to discriminate against a person solely on the basis of their race or color. Within weeks, blacks were being served at lunch

(Continues)

(Continued)

counters in six Nashville establishments. Nash continued to work for an end to segregation as a member of the Freedom Riders, an event organizer, and a nonviolence workshop instructor. She worked in the field, despite its dangers. As the movement grew, Nash became disillusioned with the male dominance within the Southern Christian Leadership Conference (SCLC), and the radical shift of the SNCC under the leadership of Stokley Carmichael.

Nash is the recipient of numerous leadership awards, including the Distinguished American Award from the John F. Kennedy Library and Foundation. She still devotes much of her time working to support racial justice through nonviolent means.

* Michael Westmoreland-White, "Diane Nash (1938–), Unsung Heroine of the Civil Rights Movement," Every Church a Peace Church, October 20, 2002. Available online at *www.ecapc.org/articles/WestmoW_2002.10.20.asp*

perpetrator. Instead, they rounded up about 81 of the blacks in the restaurant and hauled them off to jail.

One of those arrested was Fisk University student Diane Nash, organizer of the Nashville Student Movement. Describing the scene that day, Nash said:

> The police said, "Okay, all you nigras, get up from the lunch counter or we're going to arrest you." [Then] they said, "Everybody's under arrest." So we all got up and marched to the wagon. Then they turned and looked around at the lunch counter again, and the second wave of students had all taken seats . . . then a third

wave. No matter what they did and how many they arrested, there was still a lunch counter full of students there."[36]

Z. Alexander Looby, a well-respected black attorney in Nashville, agreed to represent those arrested. It mattered little, because the judge in the case ignored Looby while he spoke on behalf of his clients. He found the students guilty and fined them each $150, plus court costs. The convictions, however, did nothing to stop the momentum of the sit-ins. In Atlanta, Georgia, students attending four black colleges (Morris Brown, Clark, Morehouse, and Spelman) published a full-page ad titled "An Appeal for Human Rights." They used the ad to publicly explain their actions:

> Today's youth will not sit by submissively, while being denied all the rights, privileges and joys of life. We want to state clearly and unequivocally that we cannot tolerate, in a nation professing democracy and among people professing Christianity, the discriminatory conditions under which the Negro is living today in Atlanta, Georgia. . . . We do not intend to wait placidly for those rights which are already legally and morally ours to be meted out to us one at a time.[37]

INTEGRATING THE COUNTERS

The sit-ins continued well into the spring, with much the same result—assaults by angry, racist whites, followed by arrests for violating segregation ordinance laws or disorderly conduct. Southerners were growing impatient with the protests, annoyed by all the negative publicity and the economic impact the store boycotts were having on business. The elder black members of the movement began to feel that they were losing their role as leaders of the cause to the spirited youth now taking part in the fight to end segregation. Still, they praised the students for taking the cause to the next level—beyond the courts and to the streets and shops in cities throughout the South. Roy Wilkins, executive secretary of the NAACP, articulated the apparent shift in power during a speech in Cleveland, Ohio: "The message of this movement is plain and short. Negro youth is finished with racial segregation, not only as a philosophy but as a practice."[38]

More and more people participated in the sit-ins, reaching further and further beyond the segregated world in the Deep South. But with the sit-in protests escalating from peaceful to violent, it was just a matter of time before something really volatile erupted. In the early morning hours of April 19, 1960, someone hurled a lit bundle of dynamite from a car through the front window of Looby's house. The explosion almost completely destroyed the Nashville home. Though the blast was so powerful it shattered more than 100 windows in a building across the street, no one, including Looby and his wife, Grafta, was injured.

News of the bombing enraged the city's black community and incensed a great many whites as well. Word quickly spread that students were organizing a protest march for later in the day. At noon, about 1,000 students from Tennessee Agricultural and Industrial College filed off campus and headed silently down Jefferson Street to city hall. Along the way, protesters from Fisk University and Meharry Medical College joined the march, as did many adults from the community. By the time they reached the courthouse square, the crowd had swelled to several thousand. Nashville mayor Ben West met with a contingent of the students including Diane Nash, who asked West point blank if he felt that it was wrong to discriminate against a person solely on the basis of their race or color. The mayor did not hesitate to agree that it was wrong. Nash then asked West whether, since he believed that discrimination was wrong, he should recommend that the lunch counters in Nashville be desegregated. West simply said, "Yes." City merchants were thrilled to have the political backing they felt they needed to desegregate their stores.

Within three weeks of the protest march, six lunch counters in Nashville began serving blacks. It was a huge victory for

Nashville's black community. King went to Nashville the day after the march, not to bring inspiration to the students, he said, but rather to gain inspiration from them and what they had accomplished.

Despite the victory, no one was under the illusion that the movement was close to achieving its goals. There were still segregated bus terminals, swimming pools, theaters, hotels, restaurants, parks, libraries, and other public facilities to contend with. The decision on who was going to occupy the White House as the new president of the United States was going to be decided on votes cast in the late fall of 1960. Both candidates, the Democrat John F. Kennedy and the Republican Richard M. Nixon, would be carefully scrutinized for their stances on civil rights. Blacks were being empowered more and more each day, and their votes would definitely have an impact on the election results.

REVISITING BUS RIDES

Founded during the early years of the civil rights movement, the Congress of Racial Equality (CORE) was established by a group of students on the campus of the University of Chicago in 1942. From its inception, CORE's mission has been "to bring about equality for all people regardless of race, creed, sex, age, disability, sexual orientation, religion or ethnic background." In 1947, a group of CORE's members, nine black and nine white, embarked on a "Journey of Reconciliation," testing the *Irene Morgan v. Commonwealth of Virginia* Supreme Court ruling in 1946, in which segregation of interstate passengers on buses and trains was declared unconstitutional. Among the riders on that trip—which was scheduled to go through Virginia, North Carolina, Tennessee, and Kentucky—were Igal Roodenko, Nathan Wright, George Houser, Bayard Rustin, and James Farmer.

The riders left from Washington, D.C., on April 14, 1947, the day before Jackie Robinson broke the color barrier by becoming the first black player in Major League Baseball.

James L. Farmer, pictured here in 1964, cofounded the Congress of Racial Equality (CORE) in 1942, along with George Houser and Bernice Fisher. The organization aimed to improve race relations and end discriminatory policies through direct-action projects such as freedom rides.

Using the trip to test integration law, the nine CORE black men took seats in the front of the bus, and the nine white men took seats in the back. They never made it farther than North Carolina, where at each stop—in Raleigh, Durham, Chapel Hill, Greensboro, and Winston-Salem—their right to sit where they were on the bus was challenged by the bus drivers and police. Several of the CORE members were arrested, and some were sentenced to 30 days on a chain gang. One judge, finding the actions of the white CORE riders even more reprehensible than those of the blacks, sentenced them to 90 days in jail. The North Carolina Supreme Court upheld the convictions, arguing that the men were not traveling outside the state when they were arrested, simply traveling from one city within North Carolina to another. As a result, the 1946 U.S. Supreme Court *Morgan* decision did not apply.

Fourteen years later, CORE was ready to test the unchecked segregation practices in public transportation again. This time they would be called "Freedom Rides," and civil rights activists had learned much from the failed Journey of Reconciliation experiment. But the trip would prove more dangerous the second time around, with far graver consequences.

Desegregation's First Test

When the U.S. Supreme Court rendered its historic 1954 *Brown v. Board of Education* decision, effectively striking down segregation in the public schools of the United States, it failed to provide instructions on how states should begin to implement the desegregation process. Most school districts throughout the nation at least began taking steps to begin the integration process. Schools in the Deep South were a different story. In the same year as the court's ruling, only one school district in the state of Texas was integrated, and only two were integrated in Arkansas. Some states farther north also began to integrate their schools, but by 1958, seven southern states— Alabama, Florida, Georgia, Louisiana, Mississippi, South Carolina, and Virginia—continued to maintain segregation in their public schools.

During the first three to four years following the *Brown* decision, many southern states actively instituted means to place obstacles in the way of desegregating their schools. The citizens of the country were as divided over the *Brown* decision as they were about racism, discrimination, and inequality. Following the *Brown* decision, President Eisenhower received hundreds of letters from Americans of all backgrounds, expressing feelings of unease, anger, or approval regarding the divisive issue. When asked if he endorsed the court decision, Eisenhower would only say, "The Constitution is as the Supreme Court interprets it and I must conform to that and do my very best to see that it is carried out in this country."[39] Only a few years later, events in Arkansas would force Eisenhower to exercise presidential authority that he would have preferred to avoid.

LA PETITE ROCHE

Little Rock, the state capital of Arkansas, has been home to many notable people, including Hall of Fame third baseman Brooks Robinson, General Douglas MacArthur, and Pulitzer Prize–winning poet John Gould Fletcher. Little Rock is also home to the William J. Clinton Presidential Center, which houses the largest presidential archive collection. It is also remembered for an event that gripped a concerned nation at a time when the civil rights movement was gaining attention and growing rapidly.

Of all the southern states and all the school districts within those states, the first one to issue an official statement on the *Brown* decision was the school board of Little Rock. The statement read: "It is our responsibility to comply with federal constitutional requirements, and we intend to do so when the Supreme Court of the United States outlines the methods to be followed."[40] In the late 1940s and early 1950s, Arkansas had a reputation for being one of the more progressive states in the South. Almost four years before the *Brown* decision, the

University of Arkansas for Medical Sciences had voluntarily admitted blacks to its medical school program. A few blacks had been hired on the police force, and public spaces like parks, buses, and libraries had been integrated. That is why, when the desegregation of one of its high schools erupted into a battle of David versus Goliath—local politicians versus the federal government—many people were taken by surprise.

In trying to abide by the law, the Little Rock school department's superintendent, Virgil T. Blossom, put together a plan to begin implementing the desegregation of public schools in Little Rock in the summer of 1954. His plan was designed to integrate city schools on a gradual basis, starting with two new high schools that were scheduled to open in the fall of 1956. This would be followed by integration of the junior high schools the next year, with all the grade schools to be desegregated last. The school board countered with a proposal to integrate only one high school, to take effect in the fall of 1957, just seven days before the Supreme Court released the much-awaited implementation instructions for the desegregation of schools. "Speaking again with one voice, the Court concluded that, to achieve the goal of desegregation, the lower courts were to 'enter such orders and decrees as consistent with this opinion as are necessary and proper to admit to public schools on a racially nondiscriminatory basis with all deliberate speed the parties to these cases.'"[41]

FAUBUS'S FOLLY

Defining "deliberate speed" was the key on both sides of the issue. Those who opposed integration argued that time was needed to make changes so as to avoid any dangers that might result from moving too quickly. The argument was that everyone should be given the appropriate amount of time to adjust to the changes. But politics may have had more to do with the resistance to integration. Arkansas governor Orval Faubus cared more about public opinion than he did about being a segregationist or an integrationist. He was a politician's politician—willing to go with whatever way the tide was flowing as long as it got him elected. He cited a poll in January 1956 that indicated 85 percent of his state's constituents were opposed to integrating the public schools in Arkansas. Because of that strong and clear opposition, Faubus said he could not take part in any process to force change on a community that so overwhelmingly rejected it.

Feeling that the state was deliberately defying federal law, NAACP attorneys filed suit in federal district court in the hopes of ending the stalling tactics. In April 1957, the court concurred with the state, agreeing that the state was in compliance with the "deliberate speed" instruction from the U.S. Supreme Court. However, they also cautioned the Little Rock School Board that further delays would not be acceptable. Resentment by whites against the NAACP and blacks in Arkansas was spreading. Instead of working together toward integration, the two "communities" were becoming more polarized. Segregationists challenged those who supported integration by helping to pass laws that made the integration process more difficult and laborious; the school board continued to reduce the number of black students who would be eligible to transfer to Central High School, paring it down until only nine were deemed acceptable. Those students—14-year-old Carlotta Walls; 15-year-olds Elizabeth Eckford, Melba Pattillo, Jefferson Thomas, Terrence Roberts, and Gloria Ray; and 16-year-olds Thelma Mothershed, Ernest Green, and Minniejean Brown—were brought together by circumstances that would forever link them.

CALLING OUT THE MILITIA

Faubus and segregationists in the Little Rock community tried many different tactics to keep black students from entering the halls of Central High School. They told frightening stories of how black and white students were arming themselves for gang fights. Other stories of an outbreak of uncontrolled violence,

THE LITTLE ROCK NINE

The three boys and six girls at the center of the controversy over the integration of Little Rock Central High School became known as the Little Rock Nine. Despite the historic event that forever linked them, they went their separate ways after that year, to create their own lives away from the media and the scrutiny of a curious nation.

MINNIEJEAN BROWN went on to earn bachelor's and master's degrees in social work, and was later appointed deputy assistant secretary for Workforce Diversity at the Department of the Interior under President Bill Clinton, serving from 1999 to 2001. She has devoted much of her adult life working toward social justice and has been the recipient of numerous awards and honors.

ELIZABETH ECKFORD, most recognizable for walking through the screaming mob the first day of school, did not graduate from Central High School because all the city's schools were closed the following year. She joined the army, earned her G.E.D., and attended Central State University in Wilberforce, Ohio. A military veteran, Eckford has had numerous jobs, including history teacher and military reporter.

ERNEST GREEN made Little Rock history, becoming the first black to graduate from Central High School. Green went on to earn his bachelor's and master's degrees in sociology. Professionally, Green served as assistant secretary of Housing and Urban Affairs during the Jimmy Carter administration.

THELMA MOTHERSHED earned her diploma from Central High School by completing the necessary credits via correspondence courses and summer school. After a career in teaching, she became a volunteer in a program for abused women in Belleville, Illinois.

MELBA PATTILLO BEALS is an author and former journalist for *People* magazine and NBC. She is the only member of the Little Rock Nine who wrote a book about the experience, for which she won the Robert F. Kennedy Book Award. A mother of three, Beals makes her home in San Francisco, California.

JEFFERSON THOMAS graduated from Little Rock Central High School in 1960. He worked as an accountant with the U.S. Department of Defense before he retired. He makes his home in Anaheim, California.

DR. TERRENCE ROBERTS completed his high school education in Los Angeles, California, after Little Rock Central High School was closed following the 1957–58 school year. He went on to earn a doctoral degree and teaches at the University of California at Los Angeles and Antioch College. He and his wife have two children and one grandson.

CARLOTTA WALLS LANIER was one of the three Little Rock Nine students who eventually graduated from Central High School. Along with Jefferson Thomas, she returned to the high school in 1959 to complete her senior year. A graduate of Michigan State University, Lanier makes her home in Englewood, Colorado.

GLORIA RAY KARLMARK finished her high school education at the newly integrated Kansas City Central High School, in Missouri. She attended Illinois Technical College and earned a postgraduate degree in Stockholm, Sweden. A computer science writer, Karlmark ran a profitable magazine publishing endeavor in 39 countries. Now retired, she splits her time living in Amsterdam, the Netherlands, and Stockholm, Sweden, where her husband's family lives.

potential riots, and overall mayhem were told in court to try to sway a judge into delaying desegregation in Little Rock. When all avenues were exhausted, and Faubus was told desegregation must be permitted, he appeared on statewide television the evening before the start of school and announced that he was going

Despite the 1954 *Brown v. Board of Education* decision, Arkansas governor Orval Faubus resisted integrating his state's schools. On September 9, 1957, Faubus called in the Arkansas National Guard in an attempt to stop nine black students from attending Little Rock's Central High School. Here, students, residents, and newsmen watch as the guardsmen are dispatched outside the school.

to call out the National Guardsmen of the State of Arkansas to surround Little Rock Central High School because "it would not be possible to restore or to maintain order . . . if forcible integration is carried out tomorrow." Faubus went on to claim that blood would "run in the streets if Negro pupils should attempt to enter Central High School."[42] Faubus ordered the placement of 250 National Guardsmen at the high school and announced that the schools in the county would remain segregated, as they had been, until the threat of violence was resolved.

At her home that evening, the president of the NAACP Arkansas chapter, Daisy Bates, could not believe what she had just witnessed on television. In light of Faubus's directive to maintain the segregation of the schools, the school board issued a statement advising the black students not to try to attend Central High School or any other white school until the conflict was resolved. Once again, the school board and Faubus were rebuffed by the court. As he had just a few days prior, Federal Judge Ronald Davies ordered the desegregation to proceed. Integration in Little Rock could no longer be stopped.

Bates had planned to have all nine students assemble at a designated location where two police patrol cars would drive them to the school together. However, Bates was not able to reach one student, Elizabeth Eckford, who on the morning of September 4, 1957, walked to the bus stop to ride off to her first day of her junior year of high school. Eckford got off the bus at the school and saw a horde of white people and armed soldiers stationed in front of the building. Soon, Eckford found herself being followed by a hostile group of whites, and when she tried to go inside the school, guardsmen refused to let her pass. The image taken by *Arkansas Democrat* staff photographer Ira Wilmer Counts Jr., that day of a frightened and threatened Eckford was just one of many disturbing photographs the country saw that captured the racial hatred and bigotry spilling into the streets of Little Rock.

Not all the white people there were part of the riotous mob. Eckford was comforted by *New York Times* writer Benjamin Fine and bystander Grace Lorch. They escorted Eckford onto a bus and got her home unharmed. The other eight black students were not nearly as traumatized as Eckford, but they, too, were not permitted to attend school that day. Faubus and Judge Davies appeared to be locked in a stalemate. Faubus exhausted any further delaying tactics in court, and Davies ordered the governor to remove the National Guardsmen from the school. Three weeks had passed since the opening of school. Though the "Little Rock Nine" did get whisked into the building the next day, an angry mob outside was becoming more threatening as the day progressed. Local police were no match for the crowds, and finally Little Rock mayor Woodrow Mann telephoned the U.S. Justice Department and requested the deployment of federal troops.

EXECUTIVE ORDER

A reluctant President Eisenhower, who had said to reporters just a few months earlier during a press conference, "I can't imagine any set of circumstances that would ever induce me to send Federal troops into a Federal Court and into any area to enforce the orders of a Federal Court, because I believe that the common sense of America will never require it,"[43] was ultimately left with no other choice but to do exactly that. On September 24, 1957, Eisenhower ordered 1,000 soldiers from the Screaming Eagles 101st Airborne Division to Little Rock. He also placed the 10,000-member Arkansas National Guard under the control of the federal government. That night, Eisenhower went on national television to explain his actions to the American public:

> I want to speak to you about the serious situation that has arisen in Little Rock . . . speaking from the house of Lincoln, of Jackson and of Wilson, my words would better convey both the sadness I feel in the action I was compelled today to take and the firmness with which I intend to pursue this course until the orders of the Federal Court at Little Rock can be executed without unlawful interference. This morning the mob again gathered in front of the Central High School of Little Rock, obviously for the purpose of again preventing the carrying out of the Court's order relating to the admission of Negro children to that school. Whenever normal agencies prove inadequate to the task and it becomes necessary for the Executive Branch of the Federal Government to

When the angry mob surrounding Central High School refused to disperse, Little Rock mayor Woodrow Mann turned to the U.S. Justice Department for help. On September 24, 1957, President Dwight D. Eisenhower ordered 1,000 soldiers from the Screaming Eagles 101st Airborne Division to Little Rock to serve as bodyguards for the nine black students. Here, members of the Screaming Eagles move three Little Rock men away from the high school.

use its powers and authority to uphold Federal Courts, the President's responsibility is inescapable. In accordance with that responsibility, I have today issued an Executive Order directing the use of troops under Federal authority to aid in the execution of Federal law at Little Rock, Arkansas. . . . Mob rule cannot be allowed to override the decisions of our courts. . . . A foundation of our American way of life is our national respect for law.[44]

The 101st Airborne took control immediately. They lined the streets and provided each of the nine black students a personal bodyguard who stayed with them throughout the school day. Within days of the 101st Airborne Division's arrival, the crowds dispersed and a sense of some normalcy returned to Little Rock. At the end of the month, the troops withdrew to a base about 12 miles from the school, and the National Guardsmen were tasked to keep order. However, tensions inside the school remained, and the black students were both physically and verbally assaulted. The stress finally got to Eckford. Although she wanted to leave and go back to her old school, she was convinced to stay after being told her departure would make it more difficult on the other eight students who remained. Minniejean Brown, fed up with all the ill treatment, dumped a bowl of chili on a white boy who was harassing her. She was suspended for her actions. She was not destined to make it at Central High School. Later in the year, she was expelled for responding to a racial slur. Ernest Green, the oldest of the Little Rock Nine, made history of sorts when he became the first black to graduate from the school. The others survived the year and left the school for summer recess.

Faubus would have one more go with the integration issue. After securing the Democratic nomination to again run for governor, Faubus closed the schools rather than comply with the courts and the federal government. Some white students enrolled in private schools in time for the 1958 fall term. However, many students, both black and white, were not able to attend school for the entire year. In the summer of 1959, the U.S. Supreme Court intervened one more time, ruling that the school closings were unconstitutional and "evasive schemes could not be used to circumvent integration."[45] That August, after four long years of struggle and an unyielding determination, Little Rock's schools reopened and began to integrate as required by law.

Today, Little Rock Central High School is a National Historic Site. In 1997, on the fortieth anniversary of the historic civil rights event, the nine former students returned to the school and were escorted through its doors by President Bill Clinton. At the White House in 1999, President Clinton awarded each with the Congressional Gold Medal, America's highest civilian award. Said Clinton of the occasion, "Today, we celebrate the faith of our founders, the faith of parents in their children, the faith of children in their future. We celebrate it because we can. And we can because these nine people helped us to keep it alive."[46]

"Is This the Land of the Free, Except for Negroes?"

James Peck was intimately familiar with interstate travel troubles. As one of the white CORE members who rode the interstate buses during the Journey of Reconciliation, he had been arrested on two occasions during the infamous two-week period in April 1947, and was also assaulted by a white cab driver on the ride from Chapel Hill to Greensboro, North Carolina. Peck was going to be part of the new group of riders, known as Freedom Riders, on a journey to again test the desegregation of interstate travel. This time the route would cut right through the heart of the South. CORE's executive director, James Farmer, reasoned that it had to be done to bring on a crisis that would pull the federal government into the situation and force it to carry out the law.

The riders left Washington, D.C., on the morning of May 4, 1961. The bus route would take the passengers through

Virginia, North Carolina, and South Carolina, finishing up in New Orleans, Louisiana, on May 17. The early part of the trip was relatively uneventful except for a few disgruntled comments from other passengers. While in Atlanta on Mother's Day, the riders split into two groups for the trip to Birmingham, Alabama. Half of the riders took a Greyhound bus and half took a Trailways bus. There was one scheduled stop in Anniston, Alabama, before they arrived in Birmingham. Both trips would end in violence.

The Greyhound bus was met at the Anniston depot by an enraged mob of about 200 people. They threw stones at the bus and slashed its tires, compelling the driver to speed off to get away from the danger. The bus did not get far with its tires going flat, giving those in chase time to catch up to the bus and surround it again. In the midst of the frenzy, someone threw a firebomb through the rear door of the bus. As passengers desperately tried to scramble off the bus, the mob pulled the Freedom Riders out, attacking them with iron pipes. The bus burst into flames and was destroyed. Images of the smoke and flames engulfing the bus appeared on the television news and on the front pages of papers throughout the United States.

The Trailways bus pulled up to Anniston about an hour after the Greyhound bus had sped off. After the black passengers refused to move to the back of the bus, it was boarded by a horde of white men who beat and trampled the Freedom Riders, and then tossed them to the back of the bus. When the bus arrived in Birmingham, another frenzied mob began attacking the riders as they got off. Birmingham Public Safety Commissioner Bull Connor later told the press he had not stationed police at the bus depot because it was Mother's Day. Most of the Freedom Riders had bruises and cuts, and some had more serious injuries. James Peck required 50 stitches to close cuts and gashes on his head. Despite the assaults, the Freedom Riders were determined that their journey would continue. Said Peck to a reporter, "I think it is particularly important at

On May 4, 1961, a group of Freedom Riders left Washington, D.C., bound for New Orleans. Although the first part of the trip was mostly uneventful, once the riders reached Alabama, the buses were attacked by an angry mob. One of the members of the mob threw a firebomb into the back of this bus, which caused the bus to go up in flames.

this time when it has become national news that we continue and show that nonviolence can prevail over violence."[47]

VICIOUSLY ATTACKED

For a few days, the riders and the bus companies could not leave Birmingham. Unable to continue to ride on the buses, they headed for the airport and caught a flight to New Orleans. However, another group of riders—students from Nashville—decided they would continue the ride in Birmingham. When they arrived, however, Bull Connor put them in protective custody. After three days in jail, Connor drove the students to the Tennessee–Alabama state line, leaving them on the highway. Undeterred, the students called for help and were picked up and returned to Birmingham, where they proceeded to the bus depot. They were again refused passage.

Newly elected President John F. Kennedy had been cautiously watching the events unfold in Alabama. His brother, Robert Kennedy, was the U.S. attorney general, the chief law enforcement officer of the federal government, responsible for the nation's legal affairs. It was his job to ensure that the U.S. Supreme Court's ruling on racial integration of interstate travel was enforced. He sent justice department aide John Seigenthaler to Alabama to meet directly with the state's governor, John Patterson. After a brief discussion, Patterson agreed to provide safe passage for the bus carrying the Freedom Riders until it reached Montgomery's city limits. Pressure applied on Greyhound by Attorney General Kennedy secured safe transport. State police patrol cars would be stationed every 15 miles or so along the route, and a private plane was to fly overhead and follow the bus to the Montgomery city line, where city police would take over.

Everything went according to plan until the bus reached the outer limits of Montgomery. The plane disappeared, the state troopers' cars were no longer in sight, and there were no waiting Montgomery city police cars to guarantee safe passage. It was eerily quiet when the Greyhound bus pulled into the rather deserted Montgomery bus terminal. But as soon as the passengers started to get off the bus, a riotous mob of angry whites descended on them, beating them with pipes, sticks, and bricks. The attacks were particularly vicious against the white Freedom Riders, as the mob seemed to maul them. Seigenthaler, who was driving a rental car, heard the screams as he pulled up to the federal office building next to the bus station. While trying to help get some of the female riders into his car for safety, he was hit over the head with a lead pipe and knocked unconscious.

Only the quick thinking of Floyd Mann, an Alabama State Police officer, saved the riders from a continued thrashing. He fired shots into the air and dispersed the crowd. Later, images of the bloody, battered riders reached the airwaves. A furious Robert Kennedy, learning of the broken promise by Patterson, the savage beating experienced by the riders, and the assault on Seigenthaler, felt it was time to send federal marshals to Alabama. He readied 600 marshals to assemble at Maxwell Airforce Base, just outside Montgomery, and dispatched 200 of them into the city to protect those who were taken to the hospital. The situation worsened when Martin Luther King Jr., flew into the city and gave a fiery speech the following night at the First Baptist Church. Though protected by a host of federal marshals, as night fell, the church was surrounded by a threatening horde of whites. After mounting pressure from Robert Kennedy, Governor Patterson declared martial law and ordered the state's National Guard to disperse the mob at the church.

Having come this far, no one was willing to give up. Another group of Freedom Riders boarded two buses in Montgomery on May 24 and headed for Jackson, Mississippi. The Kennedy brothers desperately wanted to bring an end to the violence that was occupying the news headlines. To head off yet another confrontation, Robert Kennedy made a call to Mississippi senator James O. Eastland, promising not to use federal muscle to enforce the interstate integration laws if Eastland assured that there would be no mobs waiting to descend on the bus. The riders arrived safely but were arrested for violating the state's integration laws. Kennedy had ensured their safety, but could not intervene in state jurisdiction. The riders were all sent to jail. Undaunted, other Freedom Riders arrived to continue the journey. They, too, were arrested. This pattern continued throughout the summer of 1961.

None of the riders ever made it to New Orleans, but more than 300 of them traveled through the South, determined to end the interstate segregation practices outlawed by the

In 1961, U.S. Attorney General Robert Kennedy instituted a voter registration campaign for blacks in an attempt to bring interstate segregation practices to an end. Pictured here from the left are Kennedy, Assistant Attorney General Burke Marshall, Deputy Attorney General Nicolas Katzenbach, and Assistant Attorney General Norbert Schlei.

U.S. Supreme Court. On Monday, May 29, just 25 days after the rides began, Attorney General Kennedy petitioned the Interstate Commerce Commission to draft federal regulations to translate the Supreme Court's ruling barring discrimination against interstate travelers. The ruling went into effect six months later. In the end, both James Farmer and the Freedom Riders got what they had been seeking—federal involvement.

PROJECT "C"

Robert Kennedy, frustrated with the entire situation, looked for a way to channel the movement into a more productive, less confrontational direction. He believed the power to change rested in the ability to vote. From his position in Washington, he began to speak often about his belief that the true power of a free and democratic society lay in the ballot. His message was steady and constant—emphasizing the need for blacks to register to vote, to become part of the process in electing the officials that would represent their needs, instead of allowing elected officials to continue to condone the segregationist conduct in their communities. Kennedy understood that it would be a much less visible force at work—a voter registration campaign would not attract huge media coverage—but in the long term it would be a better way for blacks to secure the rights they were entitled to by law.

While the government was slow to enact the rights due to its black citizens, blacks continued to chip away at racial injustice at every opportunity—in the courts, on mass transit, and in public places. Despite the rioting and violence that erupted in September 1962, when two federal marshals were killed and 160 others injured over the desegregation of the University of Mississippi, James Meredith entered the halls of the university with federal marshals escorting him to class registration. In November 1961, the attempt to desegregate the entire Albany, Georgia, community, led to one of the largest number of arrests and jailings—more that 1,000 arrested—in the entire civil rights movement. Among them were King and Abernathy.

Reverend Fred Shuttlesworth, the SCLC's secretary, believed that by returning to Birmingham, Alabama, the segregation issue would be thrust onto the world stage as no other event up to that point had. As one of the most segregated cities in the nation, Birmingham earned the nickname "Bombingham" due to the number of racially motivated bombings in black neighborhoods from the late 1950s to the early 1960s. The goal was to head back to Birmingham in the spring of 1963 and enact

JAMES MEREDITH
(1933–)

First Black Student at the University of Mississippi

Best remembered as the first black student to gain enrollment at the University of Mississippi, James Meredith was born in Kosciusko, Mississippi, on June 25, 1933. Growing up in the segregated South, Meredith wrote years later in his book *Three Years in Mississippi*, "Ever since I was fifteen years old I have been consciously aware that I am a Negro. . . . But until I was fifteen I did not know that my group was supposed to be the inferior one. Since then I have felt a personal responsibility to change the status of my group."[*]

After serving in the U.S. Air Force for nine years (1951–1960), Meredith took college courses at a few different educational institutions before enrolling at Jackson State University in Mississippi. However, as Meredith wrote to NAACP attorney Thurgood Marshall in 1961, when seeking legal council, his "long-cherished ambition has been to break the monopoly on rights and privileges held by the whites of the state of Mississippi."[**] In pursuing that end, Meredith twice applied for admission to the all-white University of Mississippi (in Oxford), and was turned down. Believing he was rejected because he was black, Meredith filed a complaint with the courts until it was ruled that he had been discriminated against.

Winning the right to enroll at the university, Meredith's attendance was opposed by state officials and many in the student body. Determined to have the right to study there, Meredith had to endure much when he arrived on campus, including rioting and threats on his life. Concerned about his safety, President John F. Kennedy ordered the deployment of federal troops to Oxford to quell the riots, and sent federal marshals to escort Meredith to class registration. The rioting the evening before resulted in the death of two marshals,

(Continues)

(Continued)

160 injuries, and more than 200 arrests. Meredith went on to graduate from the University of Mississippi in the summer of 1963, earning a bachelor's degree in political science. More importantly, his attendance at the university became a real, symbolic civil rights victory for all black Mississippians to celebrate.

---

* "Integrating Ole Miss: Who Was James Meredith?" John F. Kennedy Library. Available online at *http://www.jfklibrary.org/meredith/jm.html*
** Ibid.

Project "C," which was designed to force the city to conform to the desegregation laws that were being blocked by Public Safety Commissioner Bull Connor. There would be no yielding in their strategy. King and the other activists planned to boycott and picket downtown merchants in the hopes of gaining attention from the press.

King knew what he was doing: His protests were designed to reach beyond the local community. *The New Yorker* magazine writer Nicholas Lemann later wrote:

> King and his advisors had a genius for generating publicity that engaged the sympathies of liberal whites in the North. It wasn't just the strategy of nonviolence and the rhetoric of hope and redemption that made King successful; it was the staging of events in order to play to the national audience. King was great at losing the battle while winning the war—"local failure and national victory."[48]

"WAIT" ALMOST ALWAYS MEANS "NEVER"

Connor had done whatever he could to prevent desegregation from occurring in Birmingham—from closing down parks to intimidating merchants who were implementing integration policies in their businesses. After Birmingham voters changed the city's form of government in November 1962 (county commissioners were replaced by city councilmen), Connor filed a petition in court asking that he be allowed to complete his term in office. Connor was determined to thwart any and all attempts by picketers and protesters to have their way in *his* city.

While the court sorted through Connor's petition, Shuttlesworth and others led pickets and protests throughout Birmingham. The intensity of the protests and the means used in breaking up the protests were getting more violent. Using police dogs and nightsticks against the demonstrators, law enforcement violently assaulted the protesters. Connor managed to get a court order banning any further picketing, demonstrations, or other means of protest. The court also named more than 100 activists who were forbidden to take part in any means of protest. King was on the list. Unknown to the law enforcement community, part of the plan in Project "C" involved taking part in a demonstration on Good Friday, April 12, which placed King in the potential path of arrest. It did not sway the young, determined minister. He had been locked up before.

Not long into the Good Friday march, King and dozens of others were arrested and taken away. Of course the media had been there to capture the full extent of the event. On April 12, several members of Birmingham's white clergy placed a full-page ad in the *Birmingham News*. Entitled "A Call for Unity," the ad suggested that King's current actions were "unwise and untimely." The clergymen agreed that social injustices were occurring but that the battle against racial segregation should take place in the courts and not the streets. Having been placed in solitary confinement, King used the time to write a response

During the Good Friday march of April 12, 1963, Martin Luther King Jr. (right) and Ralph Abernathy (left) were arrested in Birmingham, Alabama, for demonstrating without a permit. During his incarceration, King wrote his famous "Letter from Birmingham Jail," which espoused that civil disobedience was justified in attempting to win equal rights.

to them. Using only scraps of paper, King wrote a letter on April 16 that became known as "Letter from Birmingham Jail." In the letter, King tried to explain why the battle against racism should not be put off. He stated that forceful, direct actions were the only way to ensure that civil rights would be made available to everyone. He succinctly stated that "wait" almost always means "never." In other words, the time had come to make a stand against injustice. He also added that people have a moral responsibility to challenge unjust laws, and the best way to do this is through civil disobedience.

King was finally released on April 20 and shortly after found guilty of failing to go along with a court order. While appealing his conviction, members of the civil rights movement made a dangerous and critical decision—they would engage children and young adults to march in demonstrations, too. The strategy was calculated. By asking children to participate, there would be less economic impact than if an adult family member was arrested and unable to go to their job. More importantly, however, would Connor and the police want images of children being hauled off to Birmingham jails to appear on the news and in print?

CONQUERING THE BULL

The first march occurred on May 2. Connor ordered the police to arrest the protestors. But the crowd continued to swell throughout the day. By nightfall, more than 900 children, ranging in age from 6 to 16, had been arrested. The following morning, more than 1,000 children stayed out of school to participate in another march, infuriating an already exasperated Connor. Unable to control his emotions, Connor made a fatal error in judgment—and his heavy-handed action on preserving segregation had the opposite effect. Before the demonstration progressed much, Connor ordered the Birmingham police dog unit to the scene. As civil rights activist Andrew Young said later, "There was no more vivid a picture of the injustice of segregation as the confrontation between grim-faced, helmeted policemen and their dogs, and black children chanting freedom songs and hymns."[49] Connor also instructed firefighters to turn their water hoses on the protestors. The water pressure from the hoses hit with such force that children were knocked over, pushed into curbs and trees. The children were literally being washed down the streets of Birmingham.

The brutal confrontation enraged the black community. The next day, blacks took to the streets with weapons and pent-up anger. Efforts to quell a full-blown riot were barely working. By Monday, May 6, more than 2,000 demonstrators had been arrested, and the crowds continued to gather in protest. Connor called on the use of the dogs and the hoses once again. He even got assistance from the state's governor, George Wallace, who sent 500 troops to Birmingham to quell the uprising. In Washington, President Kennedy was appalled at the scene being reported on the news. Birmingham's business owners were fearful that the rioting would result in property destruction. Something had to be done to diffuse the situation, and quickly.

Without Connor's knowledge, a group of merchants representing almost three quarters of Birmingham's businesses, who also employed about 80 percent of the city's workforce, met with Burke Marshall, head of the Justice Department's Civil Rights Division. King had given Marshall the black community's demands, which needed to be met to end the demonstrations. Marshall presented those concessions to the merchants— desegregate the downtown lunch counters. The two sides agreed, and made an announcement later that day. But that did not bring an end to the violence right away.

A TIME FOR CONGRESS TO ACT

In the cover of darkness, white supremacist Ku Klux Klan leader Robert Shelton told his followers that the accord between the merchants and King was not worth the paper on which it was written. Shortly after, bombs exploded at King's brother's home and at the Gaston Motel, where King was staying. When local police and state troopers arrived, huge crowds of blacks had already amassed at both bombing sites, setting off a confrontation that had been brewing. Dozens were injured and several nearby stores were set on fire. President Kennedy felt he could no longer hold back government intervention. He dispatched federal troops to Birmingham, hoping to prevent the agreement between the business community and the citizens of Birmingham from being disrupted.

Governor Wallace was not through trying to disrupt the Kennedy administration's involvement in what he believed was the sovereignty of a state's rights. On June 11, at the top of the steps of the University of Alabama's registrar building, Wallace stood in the doorway, literally blocking two black students—Vivian Malone and James Hood—who were attempting to register for classes. Alabama National Guard general Henry Graham and several federal marshals accompanied the black students to the building. Graham simply asked Wallace to step aside. When Wallace did, Malone and Hood entered the halls of the university, bringing an end to its long history of segregation.

Kennedy was deeply disturbed by the events in Birmingham. The same night Malone and Hood registered for classes, Kennedy went on television to address the nation. He was going to announce a request he would be issuing to the U.S. Congress—the very announcement Martin Luther King Jr., Rosa Parks, Thurgood Marshall, James Farmer, Jim Peck, and countless other civil rights activists had been waiting to hear:

> [T]he fires of frustration and discord are busy in every city. Redress is sought in the street, in demonstrations, parades and protests which create tensions and threaten violence. We face, therefore, a moral crisis as a country and as a people. The old code of equity law under which we live commands for every wrong a remedy, but in too many communities, in too many parts of the country, wrongs are inflicted on Negro citizens and there are no remedies at law. Unless the Congress acts, their only remedy is in the street . . . I am, therefore, asking the Congress to enact legislation giving all Americans the right to be served in facilities which are open to the public—hotels, restaurants, theaters, retail stores, and similar establishments. This seems to me to be an elementary right. Its denial is an arbitrary indignity that no American in 1963 should have to endure, but many do.[50]

Had this president, in this time and place, finally fulfilled the hopes and desires of those who had struggled to achieve equality for so many years? King and all the others who languished and suffered during the long civil rights battle were going to make certain he had.

Moving toward Equality

When President John F. Kennedy addressed the nation on the evening of June 11, 1963, he told Americans that the time had come for the federal government to take the necessary steps to ensure that every citizen, regardless of color, be guaranteed equal treatment under the law. Those simple words, spoken by a white man who was the leader of the free world, signaled a new policy that black America had been anticipating since President Abraham Lincoln's Emancipation Proclamation more than 100 years earlier.

Kennedy's words may have been among the last encouraging ones for the civil rights struggle that NAACP field secretary Medgar Evers heard. Evers had chosen to work and live in Mississippi promoting civil rights and investigating murders that the local authorities had attributed to "accidents." Mississippians were among the most resistant to desegregation laws. At the time, the state led the nation in lynchings, assaults, and other violent crimes against a population that comprised 45 percent of its citizenry.

Segregationists were not fazed by these statistics. They were focused on keeping the black populace in what they felt was its place. Fear, intimidation, and violence were all effective ways to maintain the status quo. Evers was born in Mississippi, and despite the segregationist conditions, he never considered living anywhere else. "It may sound funny, but I love the South," Evers once said. "I don't choose to live anywhere else. There's land here, where a man can raise cattle, and I'm going to do it some day. There are lakes where a man can sink a hook and fight the bass. There is room here for my children to play and grow, and become good citizens—if the white man will let them."[51]

In his efforts to bring about racial equality and justice to Mississippi, Evers made many enemies. His home had been bombed and he received death threats almost daily. He had seen colleagues killed, their houses firebombed, and had witnessed countless others beaten because they were working to bring an end to the unjust and illegal segregation continuing to be practiced in the South. Evers had seen a lot of violence during the movement, but he also saw progress. Tragically, he would not live to see the end of segregation in his beloved Mississippi. The night after Kennedy's speech, a tired but determined Evers returned home after a late work meeting. As he stepped out of his car, he was shot in the back in his driveway. He died a short time later. In life, Evers fought tirelessly for the day when segregation would end. In death, he became a martyr for the civil rights movement.

THE MARCH ON WASHINGTON

Wanting to capitalize on the momentum provided by Kennedy's speech to the American public and his delivery of a bill to Capitol Hill on June 19, 1963, a coalition of several civil rights

MEDGAR EVERS
(1925–1963)

Activist for the NAACP

NAACP field secretary Medgar Evers had one of the most difficult and dangerous jobs of any man, let alone a black man in the racially segregated climate of 1950s Mississippi. Evers had even tried to gain acceptance to the University of Mississippi School of Law after the Supreme Court's landmark *Brown v. Board of Education* desegregation decision, which came at a time when most southern states were still not complying with the law. His rejection from the school attracted the attention of the NAACP, and before the year had come to an end, Evers was working for the association.

Born in Decatur, Mississippi, on July 2, 1925, Evers attended segregated schools until he was drafted into the U.S. Army. During World War II, he was shipped off to Normandy, France. Once home, he earned a degree in business administration from Alcorn State University. Evers was active in campus activities as a member of the debate team, and he played football and ran track; upon graduation he was listed in *Who's Who in American Colleges*. He fell in love with fellow student Myrlie Beasley and the two married in 1951.

The NAACP sent Evers to Jackson, Mississippi, to set up a local branch office there. Evers's job was to investigate violent crimes committed against blacks. He learned his job quickly when Emmett Till was murdered and he was tasked with looking for witnesses. In 1962, Evers's successful efforts to get James Meredith admitted to the University of Mississippi attracted enough attention that he was successful in securing much-needed federal assistance.

Although though he was winning the civil rights battles, Evers was also making many enemies—people who were not pleased with

(Continues)

(Continued)

how Evers's contributions were helping to break down the walls of segregation. On the evening of June 12, 1963, he was shot dead in his own driveway by an assassin's bullet. The accused killer, white supremacist Byron De La Beckwith, was tried twice in front of two all-white juries. Both times the jury could not reach a verdict. In 1989, Myrlie Evers convinced Hinds County assistant district attorney Bobby DeLaughter to reopen the case. Upon further investigation, DeLaughter and his team uncovered new evidence and found witnesses who testified that De La Beckwith had bragged about "beating the system." Thirty-one years after Evers's death, and three trials later, justice was finally served. The 73-year-old De La Beckwith was found guilty and sentenced to life in prison, where he died in 2001.

organizations wanted to put pressure on the legislature to pass the bill. Dubbed "The March on Washington for Jobs and Freedom," it actually had its roots in a 1941 initiative planned by A. Philip Randolph, pioneer of the Brotherhood of Sleeping Car Porters. Randolph wanted to organize a large march to pressure President Franklin Roosevelt into pledging job opportunities for black men and women in the defense industries, which were burgeoning due to World War II. Randolph's rationale for the march stemmed from the fact that many previously unemployed whites were working and earning wages, while thousands of blacks remained downtrodden and unemployed. The march was canceled at the last minute when Roosevelt issued

Executive Order 8802, banning discriminatory hiring practices within the federal government.

Despite Roosevelt's initiative, 22 years later blacks were still waiting for equality under the law, and Kennedy's civil rights legislation was laboring in Congress. Randolph was concerned again about the inequity in employment and wage earnings between blacks and whites. He met with other civil rights leaders, including Roy Wilkins (NAACP), James Farmer (CORE), John Lewis (SNCC), Whitney Young Jr. (Urban League), King, and his colleague Bayard Rustin (who was in charge of the logistical planning of the march). The group added other issues that the march agenda would also cover: "passage of civil rights legislation; the elimination of racial segregation in public schools; protection for demonstrators against police brutality; a major public works program to provide jobs; the passage of a law prohibiting racial discrimination in public and private hiring; a $2 per hour minimum wage; and self-government for the District of Columbia, which had a black majority."[52]

No one knew just how many people would participate in the march. But come they did. Some walked. Members of CORE's Brooklyn, New York, chapter walked the 213 miles between their borough and the steps of the Lincoln Memorial. Thirty thousand or so came via train, but most came by bus. Total estimates for the size of the crowd at its peak—from the end of the Reflecting Pool near the Washington Monument to the steps of the Lincoln Memorial—were more than a quarter of a million people, including black, white, young, old. The march was a combination of festive celebration and recognition that the event was something momentous. Demonstrators carried signs, some with catchy phrases, while others were straight to the point. Despite the diversity, there was one main theme—the march on Washington on August 28, 1963, was the largest statement made on behalf of human rights in America's 187-year history.

A DEMONSTRATION WITH PURPOSE

In the morning, activists including singers Joan Baez, Bob Dylan, and Peter, Paul, and Mary entertained the demonstrators. Hollywood actors came out in support, too, including Sidney Poitier, Marlon Brando, and Ossie Davis. Actor Charlton Heston read a speech written by poet James Baldwin. Then it was time for the organizers of the march to speak to the throngs who had traveled hundreds of miles to hear their inspiring words. A. Philip Randolph spoke first. Addressing the crowd, he said:

> Fellow Americans, we are gathered here in the largest demonstration in the history of this nation. Let the nation and world know the meaning of our numbers. We are not a pressure group. We are not an organization or a group of organizations. We are not a mob. We are the advance guard of a massive moral revolution for jobs and freedom.[53]

John Lewis, a younger, far more radical participant than the others, had prepared a speech that the organizers felt was too inflammatory. Lewis did tone it down, but it still carried the most militant message of those presented that day:

> The revolution is at hand, and we must free ourselves of the chains of political and economic slavery. The nonviolent revolution is saying, We will not wait for the courts to act, for we have been waiting hundreds of years. We will not wait for the President, nor the Justice Department, nor Congress, but we will take matters into our own hands, and create a great source of power, outside of any national structure that could and would assure us victory.... We cannot depend on any political party, for the Democrats and the Republicans have betrayed the basic principles of the Declaration of Independence.[54]

Legendary singer Mahalia Jackson rose after Lewis's speech and gave an inspiring rendition of the gospel classic "I've Been

On August 28, 1963, Martin Luther King Jr., delivered his "I Have a Dream" speech, which spoke of a future in which whites and blacks coexisted peacefully as equals. The speech, which was delivered during the March on Washington, was heard by 250,000 civil rights supporters.

'Buked and I've Been Scorned" to a crowd that felt a nerve deeply touched by the song's words. A journalist described the reaction: "The button-down men in front and the old women in back came to their feet screaming and shouting. They had not known that this thing was in them, and that they wanted it touched. From different places and different ways, with different dreams they had come, and now, hearing this sung, they were one."[55]

Closing the day's historic demonstration, King walked up to the podium and smiled at the sea of people before him. When he spoke, his words both touched and electrified the crowd. He began by telling the 250,000 people who had gathered that he was happy to join with them on a day that he believed would be thought of as the greatest demonstration for freedom in America's history. King spoke eloquently about the years of suffering, about the trials and tribulations of blacks in America, particularly in the South, with a personal understanding that resonated with his audience. Mindful of the urge by some to go forward more aggressively in the campaign for equality, King reminded his listeners that there is a right way to do so. He stated that it was essential for supporters of civil rights to stand above those who profess hatred and bitterness and not use violence as a way to achieve their goals.

As King spoke, he became more and more energized and excited. Then he exalted the crowd by sharing his dream, one in which all men would one day be able to unite in the cause of peace, freedom, justice, and equality; a dream that his four little children would be able to live in a world where they would not be "judged by the color of the skin, but by the content of their character."[56] King's speech resonated like an inspirational poem. People were stirred by his words in a way they never had been before. In closing, he magnificently stated that freedom would mean equality for all and that once united, people would be able to sing the words of the old Negro spiritual: "Free at last! Free at last! Thank God Almighty, we are free at last!"[57]

ELATION TURNS TO DESPAIR

It was only minutes before the mass of 250,000 people seemed to disperse, calmly, peacefully, without incident, from the Mall in Washington. Uplifted by what they had heard that day, most were inclined to take that positive energy back to their home-towns, in the North and South, East and West, and share the experience with those back in their communities.

But the joy and promise that came out of the March on Washington that hot August day were quickly dashed three weeks later in the center of the movement: Birmingham, Alabama. Fervent segregationists, unfazed by the march or any other achievements made by the civil rights movement, planned a deadly attack, this one having unspeakable results.

On Sunday, September 15, four young members of the Sixteenth Street Baptist Church were readying themselves in the basement to lead "Youth Day" services later that morning. A bomb that had been planted under the steps of the church exploded without warning. The church had been a perfect target for segregationists' hate—it had been used as a meeting place for civil rights leaders, including King. The explosion injured dozens, but far worse was the discovery that the four young black girls in the basement—11-year-old Denise McNair and 14-year-olds Addie Mae Collins, Carole Robertson, and Cynthia Wesley—had been killed. The bombing ignited riots, only bringing more pain and despair as several black youths were murdered and rioters had to deal with police brutality. The ini-tial investigation into the bombing was badly mishandled, but justice was eventually served. In 1977, 73-year-old Ku Klux Klan member Robert Chambliss was convicted after new evidence surfaced in the bombing. He died in prison while serving a life sentence. Two others, Thomas Blanton Jr., and Bobby Frank Cherry, were convicted in 2000 and 2002, respectively.

The civil rights bill submitted by President Kennedy in June still sat logjammed in Congress through the fall of 1963. The death of the children in Birmingham, images of hoses and attack dogs unleashed on innocent blacks, and the continued resistance to desegregation of schools were constant reminders for many civil rights supporters that they had a long way to go. The final blow that year came on November 22, when President Kennedy was assassinated while on a trip to Dallas, Texas. Kennedy's murder plunged the whole nation into profound grief and mourning. The March on Washington had brought much promise at the end of the summer of 1963. But by year's end, the country and the civil rights movement itself had reached a low point.

THE CIVIL RIGHTS ACT OF 1964

Vice President Lyndon Johnson took the oath of office for the presidency aboard the plane that brought President Kennedy's body back to Washington, D.C. On November 27, after five days of national mourning, President Johnson addressed a joint session of Congress. He spoke of what a great loss Kennedy was to the nation, and asked the help of all members of Congress and the American public in this time of transition and recovery. He recalled the "dreams" Kennedy had, including exploring space, providing better education to the nation's children, and better health care for the elderly. Then he spoke of one other dream, one he was determined to see through:

> No memorial oration or eulogy could more eloquently honor President Kennedy's memory than the earliest possible passage of the civil rights bill for which he fought so long. We have talked long enough in this country about equal rights. We have talked for one hundred years or more. It is time now to write the next chapter, and to write it in the books of law.[58]

For Johnson, telling Congress that he wanted the civil rights bill to be passed, and actually getting it signed into law were

On June 11, 1963, President John F. Kennedy delivered his famous civil rights message to the American public in which he laid the groundwork for what would become the Civil Rights Act of 1964. Kennedy is pictured here with a group of leaders from the March on Washington. From the left: Whitney Young, National Urban League; Dr. Martin Luther King Jr., Christian Leadership Conference; John Lewis, Student Non-violent Coordinating Committee; Rabbi Joachim Prinz, American Jewish Congress; Dr. Eugene P. Donnaly, National Council of Churches; A. Philip Randolph, AFL-CIO vice president; Kennedy; Walter Reuther, United Auto Workers; Vice President Johnson, rear, and Roy Wilkins, NAACP.

two entirely different matters. It took only a few months to get the bill passed in the House of Representatives, where there was little opposition. Johnson knew the Senate, where southern Democrats would fight any civil rights legislation, would be the real hurdle. In the past, southern senators had successfully blocked any civil rights legislation from getting passed by filibustering, or preventing the passage of a bill by extending the debate on the topic. In order to block filibustering, the process of cloture was evoked, which required two-thirds, or 67 (the number of Democrats in the Senate) of the 100 senators, to approve the motion. Unfortunately, 21 of the 67 Democrats were from southern states.

Needing 22 of the Senate's 33 Republican senators to vote to end cloture, Senate Majority Leader Mike Mansfield appealed to his minority leader colleague, Everett Dirksen:

> We hope in vain if we hope that this issue can be put over safely to another tomorrow, to be dealt with by another generation of senators. The time is now. The crossroads is here in the Senate. I appeal to the distinguished minority leader whose patriotism has always taken precedence over his partisanship, to join with me, and I know he will, in finding the Senate's best contribution at this time to the resolution of this grave national issue.[59]

Senator Dirksen was up to the challenge, steering his way through the senatorial procedures to get the necessary votes, and working with others on modifying language in the bill to make it more acceptable for passage.

Georgia senator Richard Russell, a staunch white supremacist, found himself at odds with his longtime friend Lyndon Johnson. Russell organized the "Southern bloc" in hopes of filibustering the bill. For 57 days, including six Saturdays, discussion on the bill engaged the Senate, keeping the legislative body from addressing any other pending business. In the end, however, bipartisanship worked in its most defining moment. A majority of the Senate, Democrat and Republican, voted 70 to 29 for cloture on the issue, ending the longest filibuster in congressional history. On the day before the full vote on the floor of the Senate, Russell addressed his colleagues:

> I am proud to have been a member of that small group of determined senators that since the 9th of March has given

... the last iota of physical strength in the effort to hold back the overwhelming combination of forces supporting this bill until its manifold evils could be laid bare before the people of the country. . . . [T]he people of the South are citizens of this Republic. They are entitled to some consideration. It seems to me that fair men should recognize that the people of the South, too, have some rights which should be respected . . .[60]

On June 19, exactly one year after John F. Kennedy submitted the legislation, the Senate voted 73 to 27 to pass the Civil Rights Act of 1964. Praise for Dirksen's efforts came from many circles. Roy Wilkins, executive secretary of the NAACP, wrote to Dirksen, "With the passage of the bill . . . the cause of human rights and the commitment of a great, democratic government to protect the guarantees embodied in its constitution will have taken a giant step forward. Your leadership of the Republican party in the Senate at this turning point will become a significant part of the history of this century."[61] Although there were many concessions made in drafting the final bill, when Johnson signed it into law on July 2, 1964, there was no doubt that it was a milestone in American history and a victory for the civil rights movement.

How Far Have We Come?

The passage of the 1964 Civil Rights Act, though a big step, did not solve all of the problems of racial discrimination in the United States. It was, however, a significant piece of legislation, because it attempted to redress many discriminatory practices that had gone on for too long. The cornerstone of the federal legislation was the ban on discrimination based on the color of a person's skin, his or her race, national origin, religion, or sex. When it was written, it was primarily intended to address protection of the rights of blacks and other minorities. Other significant features of the act included the freedom to vote and the non-segregated use of public facilities, including hotels, restaurants, theaters, parks, and restrooms.

What the 1964 Civil Rights Act did not end was the ongoing tensions between whites and blacks in the South fueled by the continued push for enforcement of racial equality.

Although President Lyndon B. Johnson signed the Civil Rights Act of 1964 into law on July 2 of that year, the groundbreaking legislation did not bring an end to racial tension between whites and blacks. Johnson is pictured here signing the bill in the East Room of the White House with members of the Senate and House of Representatives.

Alabama and Mississippi had been the two southern states that most resisted integration and the new rights of their black citizens.

On August 4, just shy of a month after President Johnson signed the Civil Rights Act into law, the bodies of three civil rights workers were found in an earthen dam in Neshoba

County, Mississippi. The three men, 21-year-old James Chaney, a black Mississippian, and two white New Yorkers, Andrew Goodman, 20, and Michael Schwerner, 24, had been part of the "Freedom Summer" drive to register black voters in the state. After investigating the burning of Mt. Zion Church on June 21, 1964, where weeks before Schwerner and Chaney had urged the congregants to register to vote, the men were pulled over and arrested on fake charges and taken to the county jail in Philadelphia, Mississippi. In a conspiracy with Ku Klux Klan members, Deputy Sheriff Cecil Price released the three men at 10:00 P.M., allowing them to drive away. A short time later, their station wagon was run off the road by another car, and Chaney, Goodman, and Schwerner were beaten and shot to death.

The FBI investigated the case and later arrested 18 men in connection to the murder, but state prosecutors refused to try the case. The federal government ended up trying the case, and eventually seven of the men charged were convicted on federal conspiracy charges and sentenced to prison. Eight other defendants were acquitted, and three cases ended in mistrial. However, after one Klan member bragged about one of the murderers having gone free, the case was reopened against Edgar Ray Killen in 2005. Killen, believed to be the ringleader of the crime, was convicted on June 21 of that year, the forty-first anniversary of the murders. Sentenced to 60 years in prison, Killen was 80 years old at the time of his arrest.

FROM A PRIZE FOR PEACE TO BLOODY SUNDAY

On December 10, 1964, Martin Luther King Jr. was awarded the Nobel Peace Prize in Oslo, Norway. The prize is awarded "to the person who shall have done the most or the best work for fraternity between the nations, for the abolition or reduction of standing armies and for the holding and promotion of peace congresses."[62] Upon learning of his selection, King announced that the $54,123 prize would be donated to further the cause of the civil rights movement. In his acceptance speech, King stated that he accepted the Nobel Prize at a time when 22 million black Americans were in the midst of a fight to bring an end to racial injustice. In accepting the award in the name of the civil rights movement and as a trustee for that movement, he concluded his speech with the following words:

> I accept this award in the spirit of a curator of some precious heirloom which he holds in trust for its true owners—all those to whom beauty is truth and truth beauty—and in whose eyes the beauty of genuine brotherhood and peace is more precious than diamonds or silver or gold.[63]

For King, and the civil rights movement, the year 1964 had ended on a high note.

Although the Fifteenth Amendment to the Constitution states that "[the] right of citizens of the United States to vote shall not be denied or abridged by the United States or by any State on account of race, color, or previous condition of servitude," many blacks in the South were not registered, let alone permitted to vote. The Student Nonviolent Coordinating Committee (SNCC) began to try to change that. Members accompanied potential black voters to the courthouse in Selma, Alabama, to help them register, but their efforts were met with resistance and some violence. Civil rights leaders began a new push on Washington for legislation to secure the right to vote. In the meantime, King announced plans to hold demonstrations in two of the most resistant states—Alabama and Mississippi.

Through January, would-be registrants in Selma were met with resistance from the police. Scuffles broke out and arrest numbers began to rise daily. In one demonstration, King was among those arrested. Upon his release, he went to Washington to pressure President Johnson to send a voting-rights proposal

On December 10, 1964, Martin Luther King Jr., became the youngest man to be awarded the Nobel Peace Prize when he accepted the prize in Oslo, Norway. King was presented with the prestigious award for promoting the principle of nonviolence in the civil rights movement.

to Congress. Pressing on with the cause, C. T. Vivian, an executive staff member of the Southern Christian Leadership Conference, went to speak at a rally in Marion, a town about 25 miles outside of Selma. When the meeting adjourned, the group commenced on a nighttime march. A huge throng of police, state troopers, and enraged white residents were waiting for them. After issuing an order to disperse, the police and the rest of the gathered mob rushed the crowd of marchers, beating whoever was in their path. One demonstrator, 26-year-old Jimmy Lee Jackson—who had run into a cafe to escape the violence in the street—was shot. He died a week later.

The outrage over the continued violence was voiced on the streets, in the churches, in the halls of Congress, and in the White House. After Jackson's funeral, the people of Marion made the decision to march on the capitol of Alabama to support freedom, or die in the process. The march for voting rights was scheduled for March 7. Alabama governor George Wallace stated that he would never allow the march to take place. The members of the SNCC and those participating in the march would not be deterred. In one of the most violent demonstrations to date, police on foot and on horseback joined state troopers in waiting for the more than 600 marchers as they approached the Edmund Pettus Bridge leading out of Selma. After being warned to disperse, local and state lawmen attacked the crowd, beating them with billy clubs and firing on them with tear gas, chasing them back into Selma.

News footage of the attack was broadcast throughout the country. Seeing innocent, peaceful people being chased, clubbed, and beaten by police turned the nation against the segregationists. An angry King led a symbolic march back to the bridge two days later. He then requested protection for a full-scale march from Selma to Montgomery. Before the march would take place, President Johnson addressed a joint session of Congress, announcing his proposal for a Voters Rights Act. Johnson believed that all Americans should support bringing an end to restrictions on the right to vote. In his statement, Johnson said:

> I speak tonight for the dignity of man and the destiny of democracy. I urge every member of both parties, Americans

of all religions and of all colors, from every section of this country, to join me in that cause. At times history and fate meet at a single time in a single place to shape a turning point in man's unending search for freedom. So it was at Lexington and Concord. So it was a century ago at Appomattox. So it was last week in Selma, Alabama. . . . There is no cause for pride in what has happened in Selma. There is no cause for self-satisfaction in the long denial of equal rights of millions of Americans. But there is cause for hope and for faith in our democracy in what is happening here tonight . . . Allow men and women to register and vote whatever the color of their skin. Extend the rights of citizenship to every citizen of this land. . . . There is no issue of States rights or national rights. There is only the struggle for human rights . . . What happened in Selma is part of a far larger movement which reaches into every section and State of America. It is the effort of American Negroes to secure for themselves the full blessings of American life. Their cause must be our cause too. Because it is not just Negroes, but really it is all of us, who must overcome the crippling legacy of bigotry and injustice. And we shall overcome.[64]

On March 21, six days after Johnson's historic address, King led a crowd of thousands out of Selma on a 54-mile walk to Montgomery, Alabama. Blacks, whites, and clergy of many faiths walked side by side, sleeping in tents and in the fields along the route at night during the five-day journey. By the time the marchers reached the capitol on Thursday, March 25, the crowd had swelled to more than 25,000. At the end of the march, King, joined by so many others involved in the on-going struggle, including Rosa Parks, Roy Wilkins, A. Philip Randolph, and John Lewis, reached the top of the capitol steps to address his fellow marchers. King told the crowd that there would be much hard work still ahead, but it would not take too long, because the "arc of the moral universe is long, but it bends towards justice."[65] Five months later, on August 6, President Johnson signed into law the Voting Rights Act.

THE DREAM LIVES ON

Martin Luther King Jr. did not live to see the completion of his dream—to see segregation completely stripped away from the fabric of America. On April 4, 1968, King was assassinated as he stood on the balcony of his room at the Lorraine Hotel in Memphis, Tennessee, where he had traveled to lead a march for better wages and working conditions for sanitation workers. Reaction to his murder was swift and violent—race riots broke out in more than 100 cities throughout the country. King's assassin, James Earl Ray, was arrested and convicted. He was sentenced to life in prison, and died in 1998.

Just seven days after King's death, President Johnson signed more civil rights legislation. The 1968 Civil Rights Act prohibited discrimination in the sale, rental, and financing of housing. Additional legislation has been passed since the days of the civil rights movement. President George H. W. Bush signed the Civil Rights Act of 1991, which strengthened existing civil rights laws and provided for compensation in cases of deliberate employment discrimination.

There have also been many more laws considered and many more court cases involving race issues since the days of the civil rights movement. In 2003, in the most important affirmative-action case since the 1978 case of *Bakke v. University of California*, the Supreme Court upheld the University of Michigan Law School policy in which race can be one of many factors taken into account by colleges in considering a student's application for admission. The majority opinion of the court (5 to 4) stated that the university's policy furthers "a compelling interest in obtaining the educational benefits that flow from a diverse student body."[66] In the world of state

On April 4, 1968, Martin Luther King Jr., was murdered by James Earl Ray. The tragic event sparked riots in more than 100 cities in the United States, including Newark, New Jersey, where firemen fight this raging inferno caused by a firebomb.

lawmaking, a controversial law was blocked in 2006, in Omaha, Nebraska, which supported a return to school segregation. The proposed law would have divided schools into districts identified by race.

Race relations are still often combustible, despite the progress and gains made in the United States. In 1992, rioters looted and destroyed property in South Central Los Angeles after a jury acquitted four white police officers in the videotaped beating of a black man, Rodney King.

MARTIN LUTHER KING JR.
(1929–1968)

Helping to End Segregation

There is perhaps no other name more synonymous with the civil rights movement than the Reverend Martin Luther King Jr. Born in Atlanta, Georgia, on January 15, 1929, King came from a line of pastors (grandfather and father) who counseled their congregants in Christian ways at the Ebenezer Baptist Church. King attended segregated public schools and graduated from high school at age 15. He continued his educational studies, attending undergraduate and graduate schools, and earned his Ph.D. from Boston University in 1955.

In 1954, the 25-year-old King arrived in Montgomery, Alabama, as the new minister of the Dexter Avenue Baptist Church. A member of the NAACP, King had already been active in promoting civil rights for his race. When he was chosen to lead the greatest nonviolent demonstration at the time—the Alabama bus boycott—he knew it was a challenge and a responsibility beyond anything else he had done in his life. As president of the Montgomery Improvement Association (MIA), King led the bus boycott to a triumphant conclusion, despite being arrested and having his home bombed. The end of the boycott brought greater change than King could have imagined. The MIA had only asked for concessions, not an outright end to segregated bus policy. But the U.S. Supreme Court ruled bus segregation unconstitutional, and blacks were free to sit anywhere they chose on a bus.

King went on to form the Southern Christian Leadership Conference and became its first president, solidifying his position as a prominent civil rights leader on the national stage. Continuing to fight racial injustice and inequality, King journeyed more than six million miles, gave more than 2,500 speeches, wrote five books,

(Continues)

(Continued)

and led peaceful protest marches aimed to end racial discrimina-
tion in the United States. In the late summer of 1963, King led the
March on Washington, in which more than 250,000 people filled
the Washington, D.C., Mall. It was there that King gave his famous
"I Have a Dream" speech. He also worked with President John F.
Kennedy on the civil rights cause and campaigned for Lyndon B.
Johnson. He was named Man of the Year in 1963 by *Time* magazine,
and at 35 years old became the youngest recipient of the Nobel
Peace Prize in 1964.

King worked tirelessly to overturn the injustices he saw in
the United States, up until the moment a sniper ended his life in
Memphis, Tennessee, on April 4, 1968. King's life and legacy
has been nurtured posthumously through many honors. Schools,
churches, and countless other buildings have been named after him.
In 1983, Congress passed a law designating the third Monday in
January Martin Luther King Jr. Day, a federal holiday in his honor.

Despite any setbacks in racial equality today—and there
still are unresolved problems—nothing can touch the enormity
of what the civil rights movement accomplished. It was the only
time in the nation's history in which millions of people came
together in the cause of freedom, justice, and equal rights for
all Americans. The civil rights movement began the redress of
racial justice, but injustice is still something that should always
be confronted. As Martin Luther King Jr., wrote in his "Letter
from Birmingham Jail":

We must use time creatively, and forever realize that the time is always ripe to do right. . . . Now is the time to lift our national policy from the quicksand of racial injustice to the solid rock of human dignity.[68]

Even after almost four decades since King's death, the time *is* always ripe to do right.

Chronology

1896 In *Plessy v. Ferguson*, the U.S. Supreme Court determines that separate but equal facilities for different races does not violate the Fourteenth Amendment.

1948 President Harry S. Truman issues Executive Order 9981, requiring integration of all branches of the military.

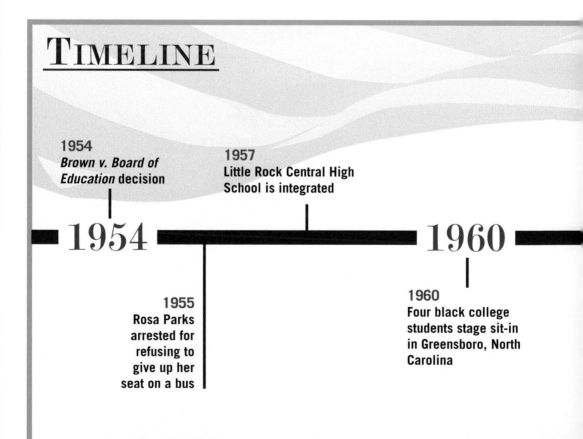

TIMELINE

1954
Brown v. Board of Education decision

1957
Little Rock Central High School is integrated

1954

1960

1955
Rosa Parks arrested for refusing to give up her seat on a bus

1960
Four black college students stage sit-in in Greensboro, North Carolina

1954   In *Brown v. Board of Education*, U.S. Supreme Court rules that separate schools for blacks and whites are by nature unequal; public schools are ordered to desegregate.

1955   **August** Fourteen-year-old Emmett Till is beaten and killed for whistling at a white woman.

       December Rosa Parks refuses to give up her seat to a white person on a segregated bus; her arrest sparks a citywide, yearlong bus boycott; buses are ordered to desegregate on December 21, 1956.

1956   Nearly 100 southern congressmen sign the Southern Manifesto, protesting desegregation decisions by the courts.

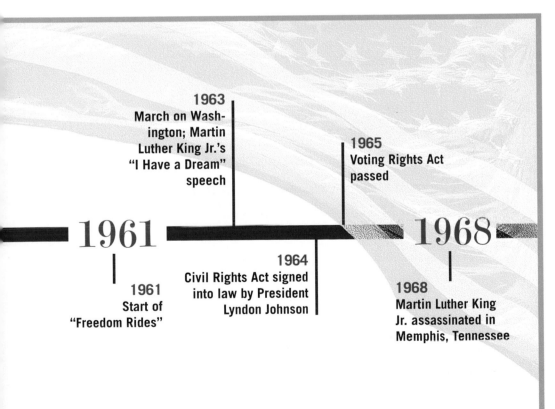

1963
March on Washington; Martin Luther King Jr.'s "I Have a Dream" speech

1965
Voting Rights Act passed

1961

1968

1961
Start of "Freedom Rides"

1964
Civil Rights Act signed into law by President Lyndon Johnson

1968
Martin Luther King Jr. assassinated in Memphis, Tennessee

1957   Southern Christian Leadership Conference is established; Reverend Martin Luther King Jr., is named its first president; after federal troops are dispatched, Little Rock Central High School becomes integrated by the admission of nine black students.

1960   Four black college students stage a sit-in at a segregated store lunch counter in Greensboro, North Carolina; protests are staged at establishments throughout the South.

1961   Blacks and whites begin Freedom Rides; several of these rides end in violence and assaults.

1962   James Meredith wins the right to attend the all-white University of Mississippi; President John F. Kennedy sends federal troops to quell the subsequent violence.

1963   **April 12** King is arrested during a protest march in Birmingham, Alabama; writes his famous "Letter from Birmingham Jail."

June 12 The day after President Kennedy announces his intent to send civil rights legislation to Congress, Medgar Evers is murdered outside his home.

August 28 March on Washington takes place; King delivers his famous "I Have a Dream" speech.

September 15 A bomb explodes at the Sixteenth Street Baptist Church in Birmingham, killing four young black girls; more riots erupt in the city.

November 22 President Kennedy is assassinated in Dallas, Texas.

1964   **July 2** Civil rights legislation passes both houses of Congress and is signed into law by President Lyndon B. Johnson.

August 4 The bodies of three missing civil rights workers who were out on a voter-registration drive are found.

December 10 King is awarded the Nobel Peace Prize.

1965 **March** Demonstrators march from Selma to Montgomery, ignoring the ban set by Governor Wallace; marchers are met by state troopers, who beat several of the protesters and use tear gas to disperse the crowd.

August 6 Voting Rights Act is signed into law, banning the use of literacy tests and poll taxes that had been employed to prevent blacks from voting.

September 24 President Johnson issues Executive Order 11246, protecting employees working for federal contractors and subcontractors from employment discrimination due to race, color, religion, sex, and national origin, and maintaining that affirmative action guarantees all qualified applicants and employees the same equal employment opportunity.

1967 In *Loving v. Virginia,* the Supreme Court rules that prohibiting interracial marriage is unconstitutional.

1968 **April 4** King is assassinated on a balcony outside his hotel room in Memphis, Tennessee.

April 11 President Johnson signs into law the 1968 Civil Rights Act that prohibits discrimination in the sale, rental, and financing of housing.

1991 President George H. W. Bush signs the 1991 Civil Rights Act, strengthening existing civil rights laws and providing for damages in cases of deliberate employment discrimination.

2003   The Supreme Court upholds the University of Michigan's Law School policy, ruling that race can be one of many factors considered by colleges when selecting their students, because it furthers "a compelling interest in obtaining the educational benefits that flow from a diverse student body."

2006   In Omaha, Nebraska, a proposed law that would have divided schools into districts identified by race is blocked.

NOTES

CHAPTER 1

1. "Slavery." Wikipedia: The Free Encyclopedia. Available online at *http://en.wikipedia.org/wiki/Slavery*

2. The National Archives, "Declaration of Independence." Available online at *http://www.archives.gov/national-archives-experience/charters/declaration_transcript.html*

3. Ibid.

4. PBS, "The Constitution and the New Nation," Africans in America. Available online at *http://www.pbs.org/wgbh/aia/part2/2narr5.html*

5. PBS, "Fugitive Slave Act 1793," Africans in America. Available online at *http://www.pbs.org/wgbh/aia/part2/2h62.html*

6. Abraham Lincoln, "A House Divided." Available online at *http://www.answers.com/topic/lincoln-s-house-divided-speech*

7. U.S. Constitution, Thirteenth Amendment. Available online at *http://www.usconstitution.com/amendments.htm*

8. U.S. Constitution, Fourteenth Amendment. Available online at *http://www.usconstitution.com/amendments.htm*

9. U.S. Constitution, Fifteenth Amendment. Available online at *http://www.usconstitution.com/amendments.htm*

10. "The National Association for the Advancement of Colored People: History." Wikipedia: The Free Encyclopedia. Available online at *http://en.wikipedia.org/wiki/NAACP*

CHAPTER 2

11. Ronald L. F. Davis, "Creating Jim Crow: In-Depth Essay," the History of Jim Crow. Available online at *http://www.jimcrowhistory.org/history/creating2.htm*

12. Ibid.

13. Ibid.

14. Lisa Cozzens, "After the Civil War: *Plessy v. Ferguson*," Watson.org. Available online at *http://www.watson.org/~lisa/blackhistory/post-civilwar/plessy.html*

15. Juan Williams, *Eyes On the Prize: America's Civil Rights Years 1954–1965* (New York: Penguin Books, 1988), 4.

16. Ibid., 8–9

17. The Federal Judiciary, "History of *Brown v. Board of Education: Murray v. Maryland* (1936)," U.S. Courts Educational Outreach. Available online at *http://www.uscourts.gov/outreach/resources/brown_journey.htm*

18. Cornell Law School, "Legal Information Institute (LII): Equal Protection." Available online at *http://www.law.cornell.edu/wex/index.php/Equal_protection*

19. Lewis Rudolph, "Up From Slavery: A Documentary History of Negro Education," Chicken-Bones: A Journal for Literary

& Artistic African-American Themes. Available online at *http://www.nathanielturner.com/educationhistorynegro23.htm*

20. Charles L. Zelden, *The Battle for the Black Ballot: Smith v. Allwright and the Defeat of the Texas All-White Primary.* Available online at *http://www .kansaspress.ku.edu/zelbat.html.*

21. Williams, 19.

22. Ibid., 31.

23. U.S. Supreme Court, *Brown v. Board of Education,* 347 U.S. 483 (1954), National Park Service. Available online at *www.nps. gov/brvb/pages/decision54 .htm*

24. Williams, 35.

CHAPTER 3

25. Carole Cannon, "Black Monday," *Jackson Free Press,* May 13, 2004. Available online at *http:// www.jacksonfreepress.com/ comments.php?id=2962_0_9_0_C*

26. Lisa Cozzens, "Early Civil Rights Struggles: The Murder of Emmett Till," Watson.org. Available online at *http://www. watson.org/~lisa/blackhistory/ early-civilrights/emmett.html*

27. Christopher Metress, ed., The *Lynching of Emmett Till, A Documentary Narrative* (Charlottesville: The University of Virginia Press, 2002), 21.

28. Cozzens, "The Murder of Emmett Till."

29. Metress, 277.

30. "The Narrative of Rosa Parks," The Black Collegian Online. Available online at *http://www. black-collegian.com/african/ rosaparks.shtml*

31. Ibid.

32. Williams, 76.

CHAPTER 4

33. Martin Luther King Jr., *Why We Can't Wait* (New York: Penguin Group, Signet Classic, 2000), 12.

34. The Fellowship of Reconciliation. "Vision and Mission Statements." Available online at *http://www.forusa.org/about/ vismis.html*

35. Williams, 129.

36. Ibid., 133.

37. Eric Morton, "The Student Nonviolent Coordinating Committee: A Brief History of A Grass-Roots Organization." Ijele: Art eJournal of the African World, 2001. Available online at *http://www.africaresource. com/ijele/vol2.1/morton.html*

38. Ibid.

CHAPTER 5

39. Russell Riley, *The Presidency and the Politics of Racial Inequality: Nation-Keeping from 1831 to 1965* (New York: Columbia University Press, 1999), 191.

40. Harry S. Ashmore, *Civil Rights and Wrongs: A Memoir of Race and Politics, 1944–1996* (Columbia: University of South Carolina Press, 1997), 104.

41. *Brown v. Board of Education of Topeka.* Available online at http://www.law.cornell.edu/ supct/html/histories/USSC_ CR_0349_0294_ZS.html

42. Ibid.

43. Eisenhower National Historic Site, "The Quotable Quotes of Dwight D. Eisenhower.

Enforcing Integration," National Park Service. Available online at *http://www.nps.gov/eise/quotes.htm*

44. Martin Luther King Jr., "Little Rock Response," National Park Service. Available online at *http://www.nps.gov/malu/documents/eisenhower_little_rock.htm*

45. Williams, 118.

46. CNN Online, "Little Rock Nine Awarded Congressional Gold Medals," November 10, 1999. Available online at *http://www.cnn.com/US/9911/09/little.rock.nine.02/index.html*

CHAPTER 6

47. Williams, 149.

48. Gail Jarvis, "Birmingham: the Rest of the Story," LewRockwell.com. Available online at *http://www.lewrockwell.com/jarvis/jarvis52.html*

49. William A. Nunnelly, *Bull Connor* (Tuscaloosa: The University of Alabama Press, 1991), 163.

50. John F. Kennedy, "Radio and Television Report to the American People on Civil Rights," June 11, 1963, John F. Kennedy Presidential Library and Museum. Available online at *http://www.jfklibrary.org/Historical+Resources/Archives/Reference+Desk/Speeches/JFK/003POF03CivilRights06111963.htm*

CHAPTER 7

51. John Padgett, "Medgar Evers," The Mississippi Writers Page, University of Mississippi Department of English. Available online at *http://www.olemiss.edu/depts/english/ms-writers/dir/evers_medgar/*

52. Shmuel Ross, "March on Washington: All About the March on Washington, August 28, 1963." Available online at *http://www.infoplease.com/spot/marchonwashington.html*

53. The White House Historical Association, "Activity: Three Voices, A. Philip Randolph." Available online at *http://www.whitehousehistory.org/04/subs/activities_03/d04_01.html*

54. The White House Historical Association, "Activity: Three Voices, John Lewis," Available online at *http://www.whitehousehistory.org/04/subs/activities_03/d04_01.html*

55. Lerone Bennett, "The March on Washington, 1963," in *The Day They Marched*, Doris E. Saunders, ed. (Chicago: Johnson Publishing, 1963), 12.

56. Martin Luther King Jr., "I Have A Dream," The King Center. Available online at *http://www.thekingcenter.org/prog/non/letter.html*

57. Ibid.

58. Lyndon B. Johnson, "Address Before a Joint Session of the Congress, November 27, 1963," Lyndon Baines Johnson Library and Museum, National Archives and Records Administration: Speeches. Available online at *http://www.lbjlib.utexas.edu/johnson/archives.hom/speeches.hom/631127.asp*

59. The Dirksen Congressional Center "Everett McKinley

Dirksen's Finest Hour: June 10, 1964," Available online at *http://www.congresslink.org/print_basics_histmats_civilrights64_cloturespeech.htm*

60. Richard B. Russell, "Speech in the Senate on his opposition to the Civil Rights Act, June, 18, 1964." Available online at *http://www.spartacus.schoolnet.co.uk/USAcivil64.htm*

61. The Dirksen Congressional Center, "Everett McKinley Dirksen's Finest Hour: June 10, 1964."

CHAPTER 8

62. "Alfred Nobel's Will," The Nobel Peace Prize. Available online at *http://www.nobel.no/eng_com_will2.html*

63. Martin Luther King Jr., "Nobel Peace Prize 1964: Acceptance Speech." Available online at *http://nobelprize.org/nobel_prizes/peace/laureates/1964/king-acceptance.html*

64. Lyndon B. Johnson, "Special Message to the Congress: The American Promise, March 15, 1965," The American Presidency Project. Available online at *http://www.presidency.ucsb.edu/ws/print.php?pid=26805*

65. Williams, 283.

66. Civil Rights Timeline: Milestones in the Modern Civil Rights Movement. Available online at *http://www.infoplease.com/spot/civilrightstimeline1.html*

67. Martin Luther King Jr., "Letter From Birmingham Jail."

BIBLIOGRAPHY

Bates, Daisy. *The Long Shadow of Little Rock: A Memoir*. New York: David McKay Company, 1962.

Davis, Ronald L. F. "Creating Jim Crow: In-Depth Essay." The History of Jim Crow. Available online at *http://www.jim-crowhistory.org/history/creating2.htm*.

King, Martin Luther Jr. *Why We Can't Wait*. New York: Penguin Group, Signet Classic, 2000.

Metress, Christopher, ed. *The Lynching of Emmett Till, A Documentary Narrative*. Charlottesville, Va.: The University of Virginia Press, 2002.

Newman, Mark. *The Civil Rights Movement*. Westport, Conn.: Praeger Publishers, 2004.

Nunnelly, William A. *Bull Connor*. Tuscaloosa: The University of Alabama Press, 1991.

PBS: *Africans in America. America's Journey through Slavery*. "Revolution: The Constitution and the New Nation."

Riley, Russell. *The Presidency and the Politics of Racial Inequality: Nation-Keeping from 1831 to 1965*. New York: Columbia University Press, 1999.

Williams, Juan. *Eyes On the Prize: America's Civil Rights Years 1954–1965*. New York: Penguin Books, 1988.

Young, Andrew. *An Easy Burden: The Civil Rights Movement and the Transformation of America*. New York: HarperCollins, 1998.

Further Reading

Finlayson, Reggie. *We Shall Overcome: The History of the American Civil Rights Movement*. Minneapolis, Minn.: Lerner Publishing Group, 2002.

McWhorter, Diane. *A Dream of Freedom: The Civil Rights Movement from 1954 to 1968*. New York: Scholastic, 2004.

Menkart, Deborah, Alana D. Murray, and Jenice View. *Putting the Movement Back into Civil Rights Teaching*. Washington, D.C.: Teaching for Change and PRRAC, 2004.

Romano, Renee Christine, and Leigh Raiford. *The Civil Rights Movement in American Memory*. Athens: University of Georgia Press, 2006.

WEB SITES

A History of African Americans in the United States
www.africanaonline.com

Congress of Racial Equality
www.core-online.org

History of Jim Crow Laws in the United States
www.jimcrowhistory.org/

National Association for the Advancement of Colored People's Legal Defense and Educational Fund
www.naacpldf.org

The Little Rock Nine
www.nps.gov/chsc/littlerocknine.html

Southern Christian Leadership Conference
http://sclcnational.org/

The Greensboro, North Carolina, Sit-ins
www.sitins.com

The King Center
www.thekingcenter.org

Picture Credits

INDEX

ABOUT THE AUTHOR

JUDY L. HASDAY, a native of Philadelphia, Pennsylvania, received her B.A. in communications and her Ed.M. in instructional technologies from Temple University. Hasday has written dozens of books for young adults, including the New York Public Library Books for the Teen Age award winners *James Earl Jones* (1999) and *The Holocaust* (2003), and the National Social Studies Council 2001 Notable Social Studies Trade Book for Young People award winner, *Extraordinary Women Athletes.* Her free time is devoted to photography, travel, and her pets: cat, Sassy, and four zebra finches, Scotch, B.J., Atticus, and Jacob.